Writing in Science

Writing in Science

*How to Scaffold Instruction
to Support Learning*

Betsy Rupp Fulwiler

Foreword by Wendy Saul

HEINEMANN
Portsmouth, NH

Heinemann
361 Hanover Street
Portsmouth, NH 03801–3912
www.heinemann.com

Offices and agents throughout the world

The material presented in this book is based on work partially supported by the National Science Foundation under Grant No. 0554651 and Grant No. 9554605, awarded to Seattle Public Schools. Any opinions, findings, and conclusions or recommendations expressed in this material are those of the author and do not necessarily reflect the views of the National Science Foundation.

Library of Congress Cataloging-in-Publication Data
Fulwiler, Betsy Rupp.
    Writing in science : how to scaffold instruction to support learning / Betsy Rupp Fulwiler.
        p. cm.
    Includes bibliographical references.
    ISBN-13: 978-0-325-01070-0 (alk. paper)
    ISBN-10: 0-325-01070-6
    1. Science—Study and teaching (Elementary)—Washington (State)—Seattle.
2. English language—Composition and exercises—Study and teaching (Elementary)—Washington (State)—Seattle.   3. School notebooks—Washington (State)—Seattle.   4. Inquiry-based learning—Washington (State)—Seattle.
I. Title.
    LB1585.3.F85 2007
    372.35'044—dc22   2007001638

Editor: Robin Najar
Production editor: Sonja S. Chapman
Cover design: Jenny Jensen Greenleaf
Photographs: Kate Fulwiler, front and back covers and Figures 3–1, 3–2, 3–10, 5–15, and Appendix B.
Compositor: Publishers' Design and Production Services, Inc.
Manufacturing: Jamie Carter

Printed in the United States of America on acid-free paper
11   10   EB   6   7   8

In memory of my father

Contents

Foreword

In the mid-1990s there were a very few people trying to figure out how connecting science and literacy might benefit students. Betsy Rupp Fulwiler was one of these. Working closely with a team of science educators in the Seattle Public Schools, she and her colleagues began using science notebooks to support inquiry learning. At first the assessments they collected were "formative"—they looked closely at both the hands-on activities and the literacy learning of students, asking always how each might support the other. And regularly, they would go back and tinker with the directions, the scaffolds, the teacher development piece—nothing was left unscrutinized. They listened and looked carefully at student work. They visited classes. They taught model lessons. At every turn they sought to improve their "product." For those of us who have watched from the sidelines it is a gift to finally have in our hands the result of their work.

Although the book begins with a report of their school improvement data, my teacher bones sent me straight to the sections that describe practices. At present, there is significant agreement among those of us concerned with linking science and literacy about what practices to support—we know that notebooks and journals, vocabulary instructions and graphic organizers all support improved student achievement. But as in all matters education-related, the success of any practice is realized in the concrete details of the plan.

Here is where *Writing in Science* shines! The descriptions of the proposed activities are done with amazing clarity and care. In the section on word walls, for instance, we learn about the importance of keeping words mobile and accessible, so that they can be used in a variety of ways and not just displayed like artwork or the school calendar. Definitions are tied to hands-on demonstration (Yes, put the filter that you used up there next to the word *filter* to remind us not only of the word's meaning, but also of the experience we had filtering that liquid!).

Most proponents of science notebooks are pleased to have students write a kind of "dawn to dusk" chronological accounting of what they did and what they noticed. Fulwiler takes us much further, pointing out that most science writing is not, in fact, chronological, and that students need to become familiar with the structures used most frequently in expository writing, for instance compare and contrast or cause and effect.

She also shows us how writing can be helpful in moving students to think more deeply about their observations or analyses. In an era of assessment and evaluation, the section on evaluating notebooks may prove especially helpful.

What I like best about Fulwiler's book is that it is real. I KNOW that each and every suggestion proposed here has been tried not once, but hundreds of times with thousands of children. And what I like second best is that even though the author has given me a very clear map of where to go and what to do, complete with compass and any other tool I might need to follow her well-worn and highly successful path, there is also room for a teacher anxious to blaze new trails to learn from the experiences of Fulwiler and the Seattle team.

So as gifts go, I am very happy with this one. I will open it regularly. I have already learned much that can be shared the next day with students. Through this volume, Fulwiler makes all of us seeking salient connections between science and literacy better teachers.

—Wendy Saul

Acknowledgments

The work that I share with you in this book began in my fifth-grade class-room a decade ago. Since then, the financial support and vision of some, the expert advice of many, and the inspiring work of over a hundred teachers—and hundreds more whom they have influenced—have helped thousands of elementary children learn to think and write like scientists and to love science.

I want to begin by thanking the organizations that have provided the additional resources necessary to develop such a unique and specialized project as the Expository Writing and Science Notebooks Program in Seat-tle Public Schools. The National Science Foundation supported the initial phase of the project, and subsequently awarded a five-year grant in 2006 to the district to develop materials that will enable us to share the program with teachers and districts across the country.

The Stuart Foundation in San Francisco funded the seminal work from 2000 through 2005. I am deeply grateful to the foundation for their substan-tial support. In particular, I want to thank Ellen Hershey, the senior program officer, who oversaw our project. Her expansive but pragmatic vision, wise counsel, and tireless championing of the work have been crucial in develop-ing the program.

The Science Notebooks Program and Seattle's K–5 Inquiry-Based Sci-ence Program would not have been possible without Lee Hood and Valerie Logan and the Institute for Systems Biology in Seattle. They know better than anyone the need to provide high-quality science education for all stu-dents, and they have been an inimitable force in helping Seattle Public Schools and other districts move toward realizing this goal.

The Nesholm Family Foundation in Seattle also has provided generous grant support through the years. We have been proud to help them with part of their mission: to provide quality educational experiences to develop the potential of underachieving students.

In 1998, Social Venture Partners in Seattle awarded a grant to two Seattle elementary schools to support teachers in learning how to teach inquiry-based mathematics. I developed the writing component for the grant, and what I learned during that project informed later work in the Science Notebooks Program.

In addition to this external support, the program has benefited immeasurably because of contributions and encouragement from the board of directors, Superintendent Raj Manhas, and staff and teachers in Seattle Public Schools. In particular, I want to thank Elaine Woo, who currently is manager of the PreK–12 Inquiry-Based Science Program. Long before literacy in science became a dominant trend, Elaine envisioned a program that could help elementary students learn to write about science. Then, as she always does, she recruited people who could carry out the vision, found resources to fund the project, and supported everyone in ways that made us achieve more than we ever thought was possible. Her mantra is always that we must "do what's best for children." Seattle students are lucky to have her working for them.

Another of the principal reasons this science-writing program has been successful is that we have worked as a team of specialists. Although I have a strong background in writing (I was an editor before becoming a teacher), I initially had as minimal a background in science, especially physics, as most elementary teachers do. I can never express the degree to which the Science Resource Teachers, the district's science-education specialists, have influenced the development of the Science Notebooks Program. I especially want to thank Kathryn Show, who from the beginning has modeled for me and so many other teachers the standards of excellence in inquiry-based science education and professional development. I also want to thank Awnie Thompson, Joseph Thompson, Laura Tyler, Wanda Lofton, Cathy Stokes, and Lezlie de Water for their support in ensuring that the writing program fosters students' science learning in the best possible ways.

All of us also turned to scientists for guidance. In the writing program, I relied most often on Stamatis Vokos, now at Seattle Pacific University, who is a physicist, a gifted educator, and a champion of science-education reform.

The writing and science programs are highly respected in Seattle Public Schools because they serve the teachers, and thus the students, so effectively. This would not be possible without Penny Knutzen, who expertly and graciously manages the myriad of administrative details involved in these complex programs.

For the student notebook entries in this book, I am indebted to the following Seattle Public Schools teachers, who not only are stellar educators but also have contributed extensively to the development of the science and science-writing programs: Ana Crossman, Paula Schachtel, Dan Jordan,

Kirsten Nesholm, Katie Renschler, Janine Tillotson, Joni Pecor, Tim Salcedo, Stephanie McPhail, Deb Schochet, Erika Shearer, Janine Knappe, Vivian Fuller Dusenbery, and Doris Toy Patin. I also owe a special thank-you to Laurie Spickard, our honorary Lead Science Writing Teacher from Bainbridge Island School District.

These teachers are part of the Lead Science Writing Teachers (LSWT) team, which since its inception in 2000, has included over one hundred teachers who work together to improve their own instruction and develop support for other teachers. In addition to those I have already mentioned, I would like to acknowledge the exceptional work of the teachers who have served as LSWTs for three years or more: Christine Patrick, Kristina Wendorf, Jim Buckwalter, Diane Eileen, Ann Kumata, Stephanie Penrod, Katherine Berg, Theresa Healey, Billie Halliday, Heather Araki, Marcie von Beck, Sarah Kuney, Althea Chow, Mindy Woodbury, Shauna Oswald, Kay Ellis, Jean Ihler, Jeannie Shu, Patsy Swartz, and Patsy Yamada.

All of us in the Science Notebooks Program and the K–5 Inquiry-Based Science Program have benefited enormously from our relationship with Mark St. John, Laura Stokes, and their colleagues at Inverness Research Associates in Inverness, California. As our evaluators and our advisors, they create an intelligent, highly professional framework in which we can analyze our work. I am especially grateful for Laura's insight, empathy, and guidance by metaphor during the development of the science-writing program and this book.

I could never have produced the final manuscript of this book without the insightful and knowledgeable counsel of Ana Crossman, Paula Schachtel, and Dan Jordan—all gifted teachers and science-education leaders in Seattle Public Schools who read and commented about each chapter. I also feel extraordinarily fortunate that Linda Clifton, former director of the Puget Sound Writing Project at the University of Washington, took a major role in this process as well, providing perspective that no one else could provide so astutely and graciously.

As part of our new grant from the National Science Foundation, the Science Notebooks Program is benefiting from the vast experience of Susan Mundry of West Ed. I am grateful for her initial insights and kind support in producing this book.

I also am indebted to Robin Najar, acquisitions editor at Heinemann, who asked me to write this book and then guided me patiently through its development; and to Sonja Chapman, Doria Turner, and their colleagues on the Heinemann production, design, and marketing team for their support and multiple talents.

I never would have made it through the years of developing this program were it not for the incredible support and expertise provided by my mentors and friends on the faculty of Seattle University's Master in Teaching Program. Whenever I was floundering in new territory, Margit McGuire, David Marshak, and Katherine Schlick Noe provided professional advice and moral support. They are my exemplars for great teaching.

As my friends and family know, I am an editor by nature. So for months, I have done battle with every word I have written on these pages. I especially am indebted to Deb Easter, editor-at-large, for her clarity, intelligence, humor, and moral support during countless phone calls. Kate, Derek, and Jonathan deserve special accolades for bringing me back, on a daily basis, to what I value above all else in my life—my children. I am incredibly proud of them and thankful that each one provides, in a unique and invaluable way, the humor and perspective that keep me on course.

Finally, I want to honor the memory of my parents. I was blessed to have a mother who embodied unconditional support and love. If she ever had concerns about my choices, she always phrased them as questions, never as criticism. My father, who died just as I was beginning this work a decade ago, is still a guiding presence. Everything I understand about the nature of clear thinking and the beauty and power of language I owe to his example. In one of a series of yearly resolutions about writing that he sent to the attorneys in his firm, he wrote: "Let us here now highly resolve that we will stop and *think* about what we want to say or write before we say or write it. Doing so is not difficult, and when you get used to it, it may even become a source of pleasure." I offer his words now as an introduction to the work I share with you—and your students—in this book.

Introduction

When I began the school year in 1996, I had just completed a week of intensive training in inquiry-based science. As part of a five-year grant from the National Science Foundation (NSF), elementary teachers in Seattle Public Schools were participating in one hundred hours of professional development to learn how to teach science by guided inquiry and develop an understanding of science content. As excited as I was about helping my fifth graders learn science in such a meaningful and effective way, I also felt overwhelmed and uncertain. For one thing, I fit the typical elementary teacher profile—my science background in school was minimal and had not involved, quite purposefully on my part, any classes in physics. Yet both of the units I was to use were physical science units. Furthermore, I was to teach this unfamiliar content through inquiry, a way of teaching and learning that I was just encountering.

Another daunting challenge was planning how I was going to teach my students how to write about science. Writing in general is not an issue for me. Before becoming a teacher, I was an editor and I have a master's degree in English. Teaching children how to write—especially within content areas so that students have something meaningful to think and write about—has always been a fundamental goal in my teaching. But scientific writing is a distinctive genre. I was going to need some help.

Whenever I had time, I tried to find information to help me. But this search was disappointing. From the perspective of literacy specialists at the time, *integrating* writing and science often meant having students write stories or poetry about what they were learning in science. I felt then, as I still do, that students typically have many opportunities to write creatively; my students did not need to write poetry about physics. What they desperately needed was to learn how to write analytically, and that required learning different expository text structures.

When I read articles about scientific writing in the elementary grades, I found that science specialists typically focused on procedural writing. Students were to write about how they set up and conducted an experiment so that someone else could replicate the experiment and get the same result. As I was beginning to learn about inquiry-based science, I thought this made sense. So I taught my students how to write procedures. I soon realized, however, that by spending so much time doing the one kind of writing, we did not have time to work on other forms of scientific thinking and writing such as observations, cause and effect, data analysis, and conclusions. And these were the forms that required increasingly higher levels of thinking and writing skills. So I clearly needed to learn more about the teaching and learning of science in order to develop the writing instruction I thought my students needed.

Fortunately, the NSF grant gave me—and about twelve hundred other teachers in Seattle Public Schools—ongoing professional development opportunities that included training in inquiry-based instruction and in science content at the adult level. In these workshops, we not only were able to learn from the district's elementary science-education specialists, who helped us understand the units we were teaching and how to teach them, but we also were able to interact with and learn from scientists.

Over the next three years, my fifth-grade teaching partner, Katie Renschler, and I worked together to apply what we were learning through the grant opportunities. We became lead teachers in the program, which meant we participated in ongoing professional development with the science-education specialists, scientists, and nationally known experts in the field. We also worked closely with our mentor, Kathryn Show, the science-education specialist who had helped plan the NSF grant for Seattle Public Schools.

During this same period, I was developing some strategies that I initially had used when I had taught remedial reading and writing classes for elementary students. Struggling students in particular need structured support in order to be successful. They especially benefit from visual reminders or cues such as graphic organizers (for example, flow maps and Venn diagrams) to help them make sense of and remember what they are learning. They also need writing frames to support them as they learn how to write different forms of text. About 25 percent of my fifth-grade students were served in remedial or special education classes, but I was realizing that all my students were benefiting from the strategies.

In 1998, the third year of the inquiry-based science training, our principal, Elaine Woo, wrote a grant so that teachers at our school and a neighboring school could work together to learn how to teach inquiry-based mathematics. (Social Venture Partners, a philanthropic organization in Seattle, funded this project.) Elaine believed it was critical for students to learn how to write about their mathematical thinking. Because of my background, she asked me to develop a writing component for the grant.

In the course of this work, I began developing strategies—based on using graphic organizers and writing frames—for teaching elementary students how to write about geometry and problem solving. A tremendous benefit of the math grant was that it allowed me to work with other teachers at my own and other grade levels so that we could determine what was working and what challenges we and the students were facing. I had taught kindergarten and worked on literacy skills with students in grades one through five. But I had not taught inquiry-based mathematics or science at any grade levels besides fifth grade.

So while Katie and I continued to work at determining what strategies and support worked well with fifth graders and the intermediate students, I turned to two excellent primary teachers to field-test the strategies at the primary level. Theresa Healey was invested in instruction that developed her kindergartners' critical thinking skills, so she taught many of the reading and writing skills through science and mathematics. Billie Halliday had the same mind-set with her second graders, and later with first graders. Together, the four of us were able to refine the strategies so that students from kindergarten through fifth grade were able to write at very sophisticated levels about their mathematical, and later their scientific, thinking. As the math writing, and then science writing, began appearing in hallway displays, parents and other visitors were amazed at how well the students, even the five-year-olds, were communicating their thinking.

In 1999, I left the classroom and began working full time with the science-education specialists in the central office of Seattle Public Schools. Elaine Woo had become the project director of the district's elementary NSF grant. Having decided that we needed to develop a formalized writing component to help teachers teach students how to write analytically about their scientific thinking, she asked me to develop the program.

The other members of the elementary science team were specializing in the different inquiry-based science units the teachers were teaching. These consisted of units developed, with the support of NSF, by Science and Technology for Children (STC), Full Option Science System (FOSS), and Insights (see Appendix C for information about these units). The specialists also had received extensive professional development in science content from scientists at the University of Washington, especially from the Physics Education Group in the Department of Physics, and in science-education reform from experts from around the country. I benefited from much of this training as well, but the specialists were the experts with whom I consulted as I began planning what the students needed in order to think and write scientifically.

With the support of Seattle Public Schools, a year of funding from NSF, then five years of funding from the Stuart Foundation in San Francisco, as well as support from the Nesholm Family Foundation and the Institute for Systems Biology (both in Seattle), I have spent the last seven years working with teachers and students to see where they are struggling and trying out solutions for those challenges.

The challenges are daunting in a district like Seattle, which has about seventy elementary schools and about 22,000 elementary students, almost 40 percent of whom receive free or reduced-price lunch. These students are not evenly distributed among the schools. For example, half the students whose notebook entries are featured in this book come from poor neighborhoods, with 70 to 78 percent of their school populations living below the poverty line. Strikingly, students in the district speak 129 languages, and 21 percent of the children come from families who do not speak English. About 13 percent of all students receive special education services.

Overall, 41 percent of the students in the district are white, 22 percent are African American, 22 percent are Asian, 12 percent are Latino, and 2 percent are American Indian. Again, however, these statistics represent the demographics of the district as a whole, not of individual classrooms. For example, two of the fifteen teachers whose students' work appears in this book have classrooms in which about 50 percent of the students are learning English. In one of these classrooms, 55 percent of the students are Asian, 26 percent are Latino, and 10 percent are African American. The classroom roster of another one of the teachers is 62 percent African American, 22 percent Asian, and 12 percent Latino. One student whose writing is included in this book attends a school in which 73 percent of the students are white, only 6 percent are learning English, and only 13 percent receive free or reduced-price lunch.

In a district with such diversity, the overwhelming challenge in developing the Science Notebooks Program was to create and field-test science and science-writing instructional practices and materials that would enable teachers to help students of all backgrounds and abilities reach their potential. In early 2000, I began conducting science-writing workshops to share the materials and strategies I already had developed. Then, in the fall of that year, I invited teachers who had been attending the workshops and had shown a particular interest in science writing and inquiry-based science to join what later became known as the Lead Science Writing Teachers (LSWT) team.

We needed to form this team for several purposes. First, the science and science-writing programs needed feedback and help from classroom teachers from a variety of schools in order to further develop and refine the programs. The teachers needed support as well. With all the competing instructional requirements, especially the emphasis on reading and mathematics, many teachers did not feel they had much time to teach science. Those who did want to devote quality instruction time to inquiry-based science usually had little collegial support in their schools. The LSWTs began meeting monthly to plan their instruction together, critique student notebook entries using new approaches to assessment, and build bonds with colleagues who shared a common interest and vision.

The LSWTs had another vital role. At this time, I began writing a supplementary writing curriculum for each of the district's eighteen elementary science units. Each curriculum gives teachers suggestions for how to integrate science writing in every lesson, blackline masters of appropriate graphic organizers and writing frames for the unit, and samples of student notebook entries with annotations about instruction and assessment. The LSWT team field-tested these curricula, then gave me feedback, including how well the strategies and materials met the needs of different types of students. The LSWTs also provided the samples of student notebook entries for the science-writing curricula. Their feedback and students' work were invaluable in the development of the Science Notebooks Program. Their work also influenced the ongoing science-writing workshops I provide three times a year for each grade level so that LSWTs and other teachers can learn about specific issues for each of their science units.

The LSWT team had twenty teachers when it began six years ago; it now includes over sixty members. They come from schools with exceptionally high rates of poverty as well as a few with very low rates. Many of them teach students who perform well below the state standards; two teach classrooms of students who test in the top 1 percent of their age group and present other types of instructional challenges. One of the things these teachers have in common is an excitement about teaching science and science writing and seeing the growth in their students' learning and love of science and science writing.

The best way to communicate this excitement is to share with you some of what they have written over the years in their annual testimonials about how participating in the Science Notebooks Program and the district's K–5 Inquiry-Based Science Program has affected their teaching and their students' learning. Sarah Kuney, for example, was teaching first grade in a school in which almost 80 percent of the students received free or reduced-price lunch. In her testimonial, she wrote:

> I wouldn't have a clue of how to teach expository writing without these classes [science-writing workshops]. It has improved my students' writing tremendously. They are able to explain their higher-level thinking in writing. It has also improved their quantitative and qualitative writing in math, as well as their journal and creative writing.

Paula Schachtel, who at the time was teaching kindergarten in the same school and now is a science-education specialist in the district, wrote the following:

> The writing program has raised my standards for what my students are capable of doing. The kids are doing more of their work on their own now, and I'm focusing my instruction on developing their scientific thinking.

Paula helped raise the bar for what kindergartners, including those who enter school not knowing their letters, can accomplish when they have the right type of support and are focused on developing the content of their writing rather than a product that simply looks good.

Ana Crossman teaches fourth and fifth grade in a school in which almost 50 percent of the students are learning English. In one of her reflections, she remarked:

> I think this writing program has greatly improved my students' writing. It has given me the support to provide my students with consistent, structured lessons in expository writing that both strengthen their scientific understandings *and* strengthen their expository writing skills. I have many ELL [English Language Learners] students and low-income students, many of whom perform below standards in basic skills, and the science-writing program has helped them come close to or even surpass writing standards.

Diane Eileen and Tim Salcedo loop with their students from third to fourth grade. About 14 percent of their students receive services in special education, and part of their joint testimonial focused on those students:

> Students with highly impacted learning disabilities almost always have breakthroughs in science writing first before we see it in other content areas. We believe this is due to the inherent structure of the writing frames that allow students to grow and write on their own later.

Katherine Berg, who teaches fourth grade in a school in which about 91 percent of the students receive free and reduced-price lunch and a significant number of children are homeless, noted the following:

> Student ideas and subsequent writing are much more organized as a result of using these thinking and writing frames. They allow *all* students to participate at some level whether they have two ideas or ten.

One elementary school in Seattle Public Schools supports the teaching and learning of students who score in approximately the top 1 percent on standardized tests. Althea Chow teaches second graders there and offered these thoughts about students who exceed most, if not all, academic standards but still present instructional challenges:

> I think that my participation in this writing program has given me important skills and tools for teaching expository writing. As a result, my students' writing is more organized, thorough, and reflective. I see real growth in their abilities to put their thoughts down on paper with organization and detail in other content areas also.

Kirsten Nesholm, who has been an LSWT since the beginning of the Science Notebooks Program, has taught first and second grades in a school in which about 54 percent of the students receive free or reduced-price lunch and 24 percent are learning English. She offers a reflection that is typical of teachers who have been participating in the program for several years or more:

> I never would have thought that I would feel comfortable teaching science. But now I love teaching it, and my kids love science, too.

The excitement and sense of accomplishment reflected in all these testimonials are common among teachers who have participated in the science-writing and inquiry-based science programs. The collective voice of these lead teachers and the specialists who have influenced the development of the programs are the "we" you will encounter throughout this book. The chapters are designed to lead you through what we all have learned in developing the different components of this integrated science-writing approach of the Science Notebooks Program:

Chapter 1

- overview of the approach
- research that documents its success

Chapter 2

- the teaching-learning sequence: when and how to teach science and expository writing in the context of inquiry-based science lessons
- science notebooks: their content, audience, and physical characteristics

Chapter 3

- science word banks and graphic organizers that develop and organize student thinking and understanding

Chapter 4

- simple forms of scientific thinking and writing: observations, cause and effect, and comparisons (includes student notebook entries)
- development of sentence fluency and independent writing skills

Chapter 5

- complex forms of scientific thinking and writing: reasoning, data analysis, and conclusions (includes student notebook entries)

Chapter 6

- assessment of student notebook entries using protocols
- an approach to providing constructive feedback about notebook entries

Chapter 7

- a strategy for developing the science writing and questions for a science unit

Chapter 8

■ a realistic continuum of implementation: where to start and what to add over time

Appendix A

■ blackline masters for graphic organizers and writing frames

Appendix B

■ a first grader's complete science notebook

Appendix C

■ resources for inquiry-based science units

Appendix D

■ focus and investigative questions for inquiry-based science units

CHAPTER ONE

Understanding the Basics of This Integrated Science-Writing Approach and What Research Says About It

The first step in implementing the integrated science-writing approach that has created so much excitement and success in Seattle's Science Notebooks Program is to understand that the approach is based on five assumptions:

1. Students are motivated to learn new concepts and skills when they are engaged in meaningful learning experiences, such as those in inquiry-based science units.
2. The ultimate goal is for students to develop an understanding of science concepts, and to do so, they must learn how to think scientifically.
3. Students also need to learn specific scientific skills (for example, making observations and interpreting data) and forms of expository writing (for example, data analysis and conclusions) to help them construct their understanding of concepts and develop their ability to think analytically. Science notebooks serve as tools in this learning.
4. Students need scaffolding and modeling to help them learn science concepts, scientific thinking and skills, and expository writing.
5. Elementary students have limited time and energy for making entries in their science notebooks, so their entries should focus on expository writing that will deepen their conceptual understanding and/or develop their scientific skills and thinking.

A second important step in effectively implementing this science-writing approach involves planning a reasonable amount of time for instruction:

1. *Teach science and science writing for a minimum of three hours a week*: two sessions of forty-five to sixty minutes for inquiry-based science and two sessions of twenty to thirty minutes for science writing. This may seem like too many minutes in your tightly scheduled day. However, by

investing time in this type of science and writing instruction, your students will develop strong thinking and expository writing skills that they can transfer to mathematics, reading, social studies, and other expository writing. Teachers in Seattle's Science Notebooks Program—including those who were concerned about investing this much time in science instruction—find that this is one of the greatest benefits of the program.

2. *Teach at least one science unit all the way through during the first year you teach with inquiry-based science units*. This ensures that students can experience the complete "story" of a unit and develop deep understanding of the concepts and thinking. When you see the increased student achievement and excitement, you will want to teach two or three full units.

This book is designed to help you keep these scheduling needs and five assumptions in mind as you begin to develop your own integrated approach to teaching science and expository writing. This first chapter presents a general overview of what your students need to learn and explains how you can structure and focus your teaching to help them learn. The chapter concludes with summaries of four studies that document the effectiveness of this integrated science-writing approach.

Thoughtful Integration of Science and Expository Writing

As your class progresses through a unit of study, the students write in their science notebooks during and after *every* science session. But this presents a challenge: How can you ensure that the writing does not detract from the students' science learning during their scientific inquiry or lesson? And how can you prevent the scientific inquiry or lesson from diminishing their writing experiences?

In Seattle's Science Notebooks Program, we discovered that the most effective way to develop the deepest learning in both science and expository writing is to schedule two separate sessions. Figure 1–1 illustrates the teaching and learning, as well as the scaffolding, involved in the inquiry-based science session and the writing session. Note that in the science session, students use their science notebooks primarily for recording their observation notes, illustrations, and data, and for providing evidence for their thinking during discussions. In the separate writing session, students learn different forms of scientific writing as ways of communicating what they are learning and pondering during the science sessions. Through the process of learning to write scientifically, they further develop their understanding and critical thinking skills.

The result of teaching science and writing in separate sessions is that students develop their understanding and skills in two contexts: inquiry-based science and expository writing instruction. Consequently, students

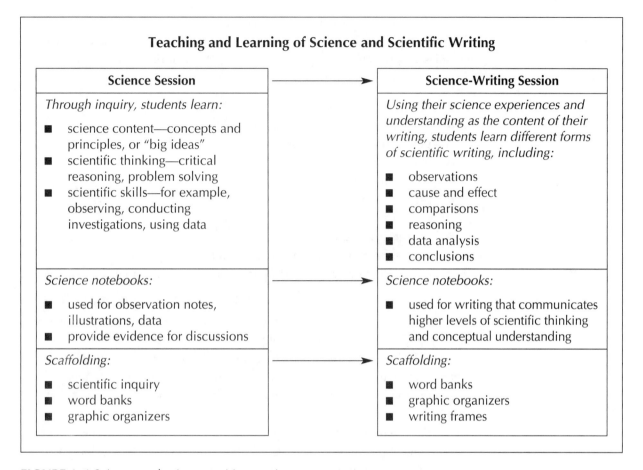

Teaching and Learning of Science and Scientific Writing

Science Session	Science-Writing Session
Through inquiry, students learn: ■ science content—concepts and principles, or "big ideas" ■ scientific thinking—critical reasoning, problem solving ■ scientific skills—for example, observing, conducting investigations, using data	*Using their science experiences and understanding as the content of their writing, students learn different forms of scientific writing, including:* ■ observations ■ cause and effect ■ comparisons ■ reasoning ■ data analysis ■ conclusions
Science notebooks: ■ used for observation notes, illustrations, data ■ provide evidence for discussions	*Science notebooks:* ■ used for writing that communicates higher levels of scientific thinking and conceptual understanding
Scaffolding: ■ scientific inquiry ■ word banks ■ graphic organizers	*Scaffolding:* ■ word banks ■ graphic organizers ■ writing frames

FIGURE 1–1 Science and science-writing sessions

experience extended, meaningful learning in all four components of the teaching and learning of science:

■ *science content*—the concepts and principles, or "big ideas," of science
■ *scientific thinking*—critical reasoning and problem-solving skills
■ *scientific skills*—skills that students use to discover the science content (for example, making observations, planning and conducting investigations, constructing explanations based on evidence)
■ *expository writing*—text structures that enable students to communicate about their scientific understanding (for example, observations, cause and effect, comparisons, data analysis, conclusions supported with data).

When you effectively integrate the teaching and learning of these components, your students develop deep understanding of each strand. This, in turn, enhances their learning in each of the other strands. The result is that your students develop scientific writing skills, and in doing so, they also learn how to think and work like scientists.

As students are learning to think critically and beginning to discover the "big ideas" of science, they have an authentic need for particular scientific skills, which also require oral and written communication skills. The scientific skills include being able to:

- create questions they can investigate
- make predictions that include reasoning
- plan and conduct controlled scientific investigations
- make detailed observations
- distinguish observations from inferences
- set up comparisons
- recognize cause-and-effect relationships
- collect and record data
- analyze and question data and explanations
- construct explanations and conclusions based on evidence.

As your students learn these skills and the ability to think critically—all of which are fundamental to scientific inquiry or inquiry-based science—they begin to understand through their own experiences the nature of scientific inquiry, or how scientists know what they know. And because they are excited about what they are discovering, they are motivated to acquire these additional skills in order to discover more and share what they have learned.

Science units typically integrate the first three components—concepts, thinking, and skills—in their lessons, but you will need to develop your own integration of the writing. The chapters in this book will help you do this.

Scaffolding for the Teaching and Learning of Science and Scientific Writing

One of the most crucial things to remember as you begin to learn and use this science-writing approach is that students require structured support or scaffolding during the science and writing sessions in order to think and write effectively about science. As you plan instruction, you need to consider how you can use the different types of scaffolding described in this book to support your students as they learn new skills and concepts.

To construct an understanding of science concepts, for example, students need to experience *scientific inquiry* within the structure of a teaching-learning sequence or learning cycle during the science session (as explained in Chapter 2). In each stage, you and the students have clearly defined roles and behaviors that are based on how students learn. Each lesson in a science unit also has a focus or investigative question that frames the lesson, helping students concentrate on what they are going to investigate during the lesson (as explained in Chapters 2 and 7).

In discussions before and after scientific investigations, develop a *science word bank* (a specialized version of a word wall or class word list) and engage your students in creating *graphic organizers* (for example, tables, graphs, flow maps, and diagrams). These forms of scaffolding organize information, data, and ideas in a visual way to help students make sense of their thinking and remind them of what they are learning. Working with the organizers also leads students to deeper levels of thinking and understanding of scientific skills and concepts (as explained in Chapters 3, 4, and 5).

Finally, as your students learn to write expository text to communicate their scientific thinking and conceptual understanding, they need to use *writing frames* as scaffolding to teach them the language and the content of different types of scientific writing. For example, to help scaffold a conclusion with intermediate students, you might provide this writing frame: "I think [general answer to the question]. I have observed [qualitative (general or comparative) data]. My data provide evidence [quantitative (measured) data]. Therefore, [concluding statements]." Younger students would use a simpler frame, such as: "I think [simple answer]. The evidence is [quantitative or qualitative data]." Such frames help students learn how to think and write scientifically and remember what they need to describe and explain—with clarity, organization, strong details, and accuracy of evidence and thinking. (Chapters 4 and 5 explain how to teach different forms of scientific writing.)

Content of Elementary Students' Science Notebooks

To promote the quality of disciplined thinking and writing that this integrated science-writing approach advocates, you need to maximize the amount of energy your elementary students have for writing and the amount of class time you can devote to the teaching of science and scientific writing. To do this, focus your students' writing energy on notebook entries that help develop conceptual understanding and critical thinking within the context of their investigations. For example, students do not need to spend time writing responses to generic questions such as "What did you learn today?" (This would be part of a science learning-log approach.) Instead, they should respond to specific, carefully crafted questions that focus their writing on their observations, data analysis, scientific reasoning, and conclusions.

To focus the writing even further, have your students write about only the concepts and thinking involved in their investigations. They all should *talk* in more open-ended ways about their questions and thinking that go beyond the investigation because this is an essential part of scientific inquiry. Other science-notebook approaches have a different emphasis. They advocate that students also should write about their open-ended, disconnected thinking and questioning that go beyond their investigations. Scientists, of course, think in these ways, too. But this integrated science-writing approach is structured so that students concentrate on learning the more disciplined forms of scientific thinking and writing.

Another distinctive feature of this approach is that except in rare, specific instances, students do not write about materials and investigation procedures. Procedural writing requires a great deal of time and energy yet involves only lower-level thinking and writing skills (as explained in Chapter 2). Your students should spend concentrated time *planning and discussing* their procedures, including how different variables can affect test results. These are fundamental elements of scientific inquiry. But elementary students do not need to spend their limited time and energy writing up their procedures so that someone else can replicate the experiment. The more valuable goal of this focused science-writing approach is for students to use their time in learning how to write about their higher-level thinking and conceptual understanding.

Research

Four studies of the Science Notebooks Program (described in the introduction) document the success of this integrated science-writing approach within Seattle Public Schools. The studies have analyzed the approach from various perspectives over the first six years of the program. Although the studies could not control for the many variables that can affect student performance, the trends in the cumulative qualitative and quantitative data in the four studies provide strong evidence of the effectiveness of this approach.

Inverness Research Associates of Inverness, California, evaluated the Science Notebooks Program from 2000 through 2005 through a grant from the Stuart Foundation in San Francisco. In 2006, the National Science Foundation (NSF) awarded the Seattle Public Schools a grant to develop a model of the Science Notebooks Program that other school districts could implement to meet their needs. Inverness is evaluating and conducting research about this NSF project. They also evaluate other NSF math and science projects as well as the National Writing Project.

In 2002, during the initial development of the Science Notebooks Program, Inverness conducted a study to determine the extent to which and in what ways the science-writing approach helps teachers improve their teaching of both science and expository writing in terms of the goals of the approach. Inverness sampled notebooks from the classrooms of Lead Science Writing Teachers (LSWTs), full-time elementary teachers who participate in ongoing science-writing classes and also meet monthly to plan science-writing instruction and critique student work. (Some of this work is described in the introduction and in Chapter 6.) The researchers also interviewed these teachers.

One aspect of this first study addressed teachers' beliefs about how participating in the program had affected their classroom practices. The responses were extremely positive about the program's benefits (Stokes, St. John, and Fyfe 2002, 7):

> Teachers state strongly that the Expository Writing and Science Notebooks Program gives them the resources and strategies they need in order to improve their teaching of the hands-on science kits adopted by the elementary science program, and to improve their teaching of writing. The approach also helps them assess student learning and monitor their own teaching.

What was even more important to these teachers were the ways in which they felt their students had benefited in both their learning of science and expository writing (Stokes, St. John, and Fyfe 2002, 10):

> Teachers believe strongly that the program's approach to writing in science notebooks helps their students learn both concepts and skills in science, and learn to write in ways that deeply engage students and that also reflect the rigor of science as a discipline. Teachers believe the approach is especially powerful for English Language Learners and others for whom learning is a struggle. Teachers also believe that the skills build cumulatively, are lasting, and support students' learning across the curriculum.

A second part of this research included a study of 150 notebooks from first-, third-, and fifth-grade students in fifteen classrooms in thirteen elementary schools. The notebooks were randomly selected to reflect the proportion in each classroom of students served in the English language learners (ELL) and special education programs. The school sample also included more schools with higher concentrations of low-socioeconomic-status and ELL students in order to determine if such students did benefit, as the interviewed teachers believed, from the program's approach. Two groups of readers then rated the notebooks: a group of Seattle's LSWTs and a group of experts who were independent of the program but were elementary classroom teachers with extensive experience in teaching science and science writing, professional development leaders involved in science-education reform, and researchers of science and/or writing education.

The results of the reading by the independent experts, who were unfamiliar with the project, were particularly significant in that they compared the notebooks with "typical" elementary science notebooks they had seen throughout the country (Stokes, St. John, and Fyfe 2002, 40):

> The raters said that the Seattle notebooks stand out from notebooks they have seen in other programs because they contain a greater amount of student writing overall, they reflect a much more deliberate and systematic approach to developing students' writing and science

skills, and they offer students greater opportunities than typical science notebooks to formulate and express their ideas in science.

In 2003, Inverness conducted a second study to determine how effective the approach is in terms of meeting goals of Seattle Public Schools administrators and people involved in the broader science-education reform community outside the district. The study included a similar sampling of notebooks as in the earlier study, and the reviewers this time were district administrators and outside experts from various areas of education—elementary classroom teachers, school administrators, professors in science education, and leaders of initiatives for policy and education reform. The researchers also surveyed almost six hundred Seattle teachers, half of whom had taken some science-writing workshops and half of whom had not.

The study reported positive findings about the effectiveness of the approach in three important areas (Stokes, Hirabayashi, and Ramage 2003, ii):

Contribution to Student Learning

The student notebooks show evidence of a systematic approach to teaching in which writing improves students' learning of science concepts and skills, and in which science serves as a potent context for the development of writing. Independent experts judge that the student work in science notebooks is, on the whole, more sophisticated in quality, and reflective of greater rigor and a higher level of learning of both science and writing, than is typical in science programs in other schools and districts that use similar science units.

Enhancement of Teacher Practice and District Programs

The curriculum strand, teaching practices, and professional development classes of the Seattle Expository Writing and Science Notebooks Program appear to be adding substantial value to teachers' repertoires of classroom practice in the teaching of science and writing in science. The Writing program thus enhances to a significant degree the district's elementary science program, and it helps bolster the district's literacy program, including the extent to which those programs help students meet state standards.

Implementation at a Significant Scale

Participants in the Expository Writing and Science Notebooks Program spend more time teaching science, teach more writing in science, have higher expectations for students with special needs, and follow the district's science curriculum more consistently than teachers who have little or no experience with the Expository Writing program.

The third Inverness study, conducted in 2005, focused on how the approach works with teachers who have had minimal hours of professional development—only two or three workshops, which is a total of four and one-half hours of training—over two years. These teachers are more "typical" because they participate in only a few workshops (in which they receive supplementary science-writing curriculum) and are potentially less serious in their implementation of the approach than the LSWTs, who participate extensively in workshops in addition to monthly higher-level professional development opportunities. As in the first two studies, LSWTs and independent experts reviewed and rated science notebooks.

This study supported the findings in the two earlier studies, and virtually all the reviewers agreed that "there are clearly more benefits to students than detriments" when teachers only partially implement the approach according to the program's intended goals (Stokes, Mitchell, and Ramage 2005, iii).

Also in 2005, the National Center for Research on Evaluation, Standards, and Student Testing (CRESST) at the University of California at Los Angeles conducted a quantitative study of the effects of the Science Notebooks Program under a grant from the Stuart Foundation. In part, this study examined the relationship between teacher participation in the Science Notebooks Program's professional development and fifth-grade student performance on the science portion of the state's high-stakes assessment, the Washington Assessment of Student Learning or WASL. (In the elementary schools, only fifth graders take the science WASL.)

CRESST reasoned that to be considered a serious participant in the Science Notebooks Program, and thus a potentially serious implementer of the approach, a teacher would have attended at least the four science-writing workshops for her grade level. This level of participation would require seven and one-half hours of classes over the course of two years and would include a unit-specific writing curriculum for each of the three district-adopted science units at her grade level. (Chapter 7 describes how to develop writing instruction and materials for your science units.)

The sample of fifth-grade teachers who met this level of participation was small. (The workshops are not mandatory.) But the results still show evidence that the science-writing program positively affects student learning. The study found, for example, that "students in classrooms taught by 5th grade teachers high in Science Notebook professional development significantly outperformed other students." Fifth graders whose fourth- and fifth-grade teachers had high participation in the Science Notebooks professional development scored even higher (Herman 2005, 22, 23).

In addition, the study reported findings of significance for schools with large populations of students with low socioeconomic status (SES). The study found (Herman 2005, 23):

> a significant relationship between classroom SES level and prior year teacher effects. The expected difference between students taught in the fourth grade by teachers high in Science Notebook professional

development and those taught by other teachers is larger for low SES classrooms than for high SES classrooms. This finding suggests that extended participation in the Science Notebook Program, as defined by prior year teachers' involvement in program professional development, is more important for low SES classrooms than for higher SES classrooms and that classrooms (and by extension schools) where there are the highest concentrations of economically poor students show particular benefits from at least two years of program participation.

The CRESST and Inverness studies together provide strong evidence that teachers who implement the science-writing approach of Seattle's Science Notebooks Program can improve their teaching practices in both inquiry-based science and expository writing. This book is designed to help you implement this approach in your own classroom.

Essential Guidelines for Using the Approach with Your Students

As you learn more about the strategies and begin to implement them in your teaching, remember these four essential guidelines:

1. Focus the teaching and learning on developing students' scientific thinking and understanding of science concepts.
2. Teach students scientific and expository writing skills so that students can deepen their thinking and conceptual understanding and learn a variety of forms of scientific writing.
3. Make science notebooks an integral part of the teaching and learning of science and expository writing.
4. Provide modeling and scaffolding—scientific inquiry, word bank, graphic organizers, and writing frames—for all parts of the teaching and learning in the science and writing sessions.

As the research has shown, when you use this disciplined, structured approach, your students—including those who come from low socioeconomic backgrounds and those who are learning English or have other special needs—will develop strong critical thinking skills and understanding of science concepts as well as proficient science and expository writing skills. And, as hundreds of teachers in our program will tell you, the best part of all is that your students will love science and feel proud of their work as scientists, and you will feel good about your teaching.

References

Herman, Joan L. 2005. "Seattle School District—Effects of Expository Writing and Science Notebooks Program: Using Existing Data to Explore Program Effects on Students' Science Learning." Report for the Stuart Foundation, San Francisco. Los Angeles: National Center for Research on Evaluation, Standards, and Student Testing (CRESST), University of California.

Stokes, Laura, Judy Hirabayashi, and Katherine Ramage. 2003. "Writing for Science and Science for Writing: The Seattle Elementary Expository Writing and Science Notebooks Program as a Model for Classrooms and Districts." Posted at www.inverness-research.org/reports.html. Inverness, CA: Inverness Research Associates.

Stokes, Laura, Heather Mitchell, and Katherine Ramage. 2005. "Learning to Teach Science with Writing: Implementation of the Seattle Elementary Expository Writing and Science Notebooks Program in Typical Classrooms." Posted at www.inverness-research.org/reports.html. Inverness, CA: Inverness Research Associates.

Stokes, Laura, Mark St. John, and Jo Fyfe. 2002. "Writing for Science, Science for Writing: A Study of the Seattle Elementary Science Expository Writing and Science Notebooks Program." Posted at www.inverness-research.org/reports.html. Inverness, CA: Inverness Research Associates.

CHAPTER TWO

Using Science Notebooks in Integrating Science and Expository Writing Instruction

To integrate science and expository writing instruction in meaningful and effective ways, you need to balance your students' science experiences with writing instruction. We have found in years of working with hundreds of elementary teachers in the Science Notebooks Program that one of the greatest challenges to achieving effective integration of the two domains is knowing when and how to focus on science and when and how to focus on expository writing so that the two domains enhance, rather than detract from, each other. We have always used science notebooks as a tool for integrating science and writing. Students use them for recording observation notes and data, providing evidence during discussions, and writing about their higher-level thinking and understanding. But too often, teachers and students became more focused on producing something in the notebooks than in engaging students' minds in the scientific investigations.

This chapter will help you avoid these problems. It explains solutions we have found for this challenge as well as specific information about the audience, content, and physical characteristics of science notebooks in this integrated science-writing approach.

Scheduling Science and Science-Writing Sessions

When we first started this science-writing program, we expected students to be able to write about their thinking during the science session. But students were not processing their thinking as they wrote. When we included writing instruction so that students could learn to write in more complex ways, students did not have enough time to work with the materials and conduct their investigations. Consequently, the learning of both science and expository writing suffered, and many students resented the writing because it interfered with their experiences in the investigations.

Since then, our teachers routinely schedule two separate sessions, one for science and one for writing. In the primary grades, the teaching-learning sequence of a science session takes from forty-five to fifty minutes; in the intermediate grades, the science session requires from fifty to seventy-five minutes depending on the lesson and time available.

In a separate writing session of about twenty to thirty minutes—in what is actually an integrated literacy block—students revisit their thinking about what they have discovered, then learn how to write in whatever form is appropriate. This writing session occurs later in the day of the science session or sometime the next day. Initially, new teachers in our program are concerned about spending this much time "on science" when their scheduling must accommodate so many competing needs. But those who have allocated their science and science-writing instruction in this way are thrilled with the unanticipated benefits. Students develop strong conceptual understanding of science, scientific thinking, scientific skills, and expository writing skills. Furthermore, they apply these skills in mathematics and other content areas as well as in written responses in reading.

Science Session: The Teaching-Learning Sequence

The typical teaching-learning sequence of science instruction shown in Figure 2–1 provides a sequential framework for you to use in understanding and planning when your students should write in their notebooks, what type of written communication they can use at different times during the science session, and what you need to do to support them. (This book is not intended to explain inquiry-based science, but good science instruction—including having students actively engage in learning and using the scientific skills listed in Chapter 1—is critical to effective integration of the teaching and learning of science and writing.) This sequence, which in inquiry-based science often is called a learning cycle, is a way of teaching science that is based on research about how children learn. Teacher's guides and other publications refer to the phases of this sequence with similar names. In this brief description, the sequence includes four stages of science instruction and learning: engagement, active investigation, shared reflection, and application.

Stage One: Engagement
When it is time for science, your students should automatically take out their science notebook and write the day's date *in numerals* at the top of the next blank page. (We have found that kindergartners can write the numerals, too, if you model how to do it. Do not worry about how the date looks.) In this first stage of the teaching-learning sequence, you need to engage your students in what they are going to be thinking about and investigating,

	Science Session: The Teaching-Learning Sequence and Students' Use of Science Notebooks			
Stages	**1. Engagement**	**2. Active Investigation**	**3. Shared Reflection**	**4. Application**
Teacher	Models making tables, notes, data entries, illustrations, diagrams.	Works with groups: ■ asks questions ■ models language, thinking ■ addresses misconceptions.	Models making tables, graphs of class data, graphic organizers. Introduces new words to word bank. Models language, thinking.	Leads discussion to connect lesson with real world or further investigations.
Students	Write: ■ date ■ focus or investigative question ■ prediction with reasoning ■ table.	Record data. Take notes. Make illustrations, diagrams.	Use notebooks to provide data for class results, evidence for own reasoning, explanations, conclusions.	May use notebooks to provide ideas, questions.

FIGURE 2–1 The teaching-learning sequence and science notebooks

using questioning and brainstorming to help them make connections with their prior knowledge or previous investigations.

At an appropriate time during this initial stage, begin to focus the discussion on what your students will be investigating when they work with concrete materials in the second stage, active investigation. As the discussion becomes more focused, either provide a question that directs the students toward what they should be thinking about as they explore with the materials or guide students in writing a question to investigate. These focus or investigative questions are a vital component of both effective science and science-writing experiences because the questions give teachers and students a focal point for their investigation, their thinking, and their talking. (Chapter 7 explains how to develop these questions for a science unit.) The following are some examples:

■ What do you notice about the body of a land snail? (*Animals Two by Two*, a kindergarten unit published by Full Option Science System or FOSS)

■ What do platys do when you put a tunnel in the aquarium? (*Animals Two by Two*)

- What are the properties of a good bouncer? (*Balls and Ramps*, a first-grade unit published by Insights)
- What happens to the brightness of a bulb when you change the length of wire in a closed circuit? (*Circuits and Pathways*, a fourth-grade unit published by Insights)
- How does greater water flow affect erosion and deposition in the stream table? (*Land and Water*, a fourth-grade unit published by Science and Technology for Children or STC)

When you introduce or, as a class, create the focus or investigative question, students write it in their notebook. For young students, you can type and copy the question before the science session. Then give students a copy of the question, either on a strip of paper or on an address label, so they easily can glue or attach it below the day's date in their science notebook. After students have entered the question in their notebook, ask them to circle the key words in the question. Next, lead a class discussion about which words the students think are important and why. For example, in the question above—What are the properties of a good bouncer?—students would discuss the meaning of the words *properties*, *bouncer*, and *good*, as well as the question mark. This process helps students focus on the question, teaches them to read a question carefully, and improves their reading skills. The question then serves as a title for their notebook entry.

In a more complex investigative question for intermediate lessons, students would identify variables. Using the investigative question, How does greater water flow affect erosion and deposition in the stream table? you would want students to identify *water flow*, which is the variable they are going to change or manipulate by making it *greater*. To determine if changing or manipulating the variable is going to have an effect on *erosion* and *deposition*, students would have to observe and measure these responding variables. Students also would need to note that *stream table* is an important term because it is where the investigation is being conducted, and it is a model of a natural stream system.

After discussing the focus or investigative question during the engagement stage, students may need to do or learn several other things, depending on the lesson. If they are going to conduct a controlled investigation, they need to record a prediction for the question in their science notebook. Before they write their prediction, you need to model how they can provide reasoning for their prediction by using *because*. For example, your modeling of a prediction for the earlier question might be, "I predict that greater water flow will cause more erosion and deposition in the stream table. I think this because _____ ."

You also may need to model how to create a table and write observation notes, record quantitative (measured) data, or make a diagram or simple illustration of what students will be observing. Involve students in this process so that you are not telling them what they are going to be observing.

(Chapter 4 explains how to model creating tables, taking notes, drawing scientific illustrations, and making simple diagrams.)

If students need to plan a controlled investigation, they will do so in an extended version of this stage, which, depending on the grade level, might take the entire science session for that day. To help plan all the components of an investigation (for example, creating the question, then determining the variable that they will change or manipulate, the variables that they must keep the same or control, and the variables that they will measure and/or observe), students can use the Planning Your Own Scientific Investigation template shown in Chapter 3 and Appendix A. For class discussions of this planning, make lists of the components on wall charts so students have another scaffolding while discussing the planning as a class (see Figure 2–2).

As explained in Chapter 1, the Science Notebooks Program does not require students to write up their investigation plans in their science notebooks because this is low-level writing that uses up valuable time and energy that we would rather have them invest in developing higher-level thinking and writing skills. However, it is essential to their science education

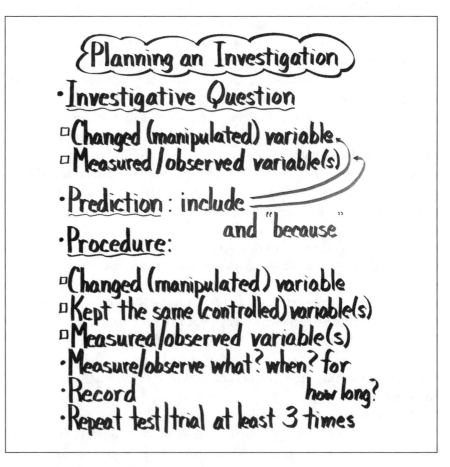

FIGURE 2–2 Wall chart for planning an investigation

that students know how to plan and conduct investigations, and also learn about the different kinds of variables and how they can affect investigation outcomes. Using the planning template helps students learn these essential elements of an investigation, which will be important as they discuss, analyze, interpret, and write about the investigation outcomes.

Stage Two: Active Investigation

In the active investigation stage, your students' minds are focused on a question as they begin to work with concrete materials to collect some type of data (observations and/or measured data). During this second stage, as students are working with concrete materials, they should do only minimal writing so they are not distracted from the science by the demands of the writing. If they are collecting quantitative (measured) data, they should record their results in their own notebook throughout this stage. If they are recording simple observation notes, they can do that after they have explored with the materials for a while. If they need to make detailed scientific illustrations, they can draw during the middle and end of this stage, depending on the lesson.

While students are investigating, visit the different groups. Facilitate discussion among team members. Ask questions, and if students have misconceptions, ask more questions to help them reflect about their ideas and thinking. Also model scientific thinking and ask students to speak and think like scientists (for example, by using scientific words such as *data* and *evidence*, and providing evidence for their claims).

Be sure to allow enough time during this active investigation stage for students to investigate with the materials and to discuss with the members of their investigation team what they are observing and discovering. Often, student misconceptions and inaccurate and/or inadequate content in the notebook writing are due to lack of time and purposeful talking during this stage. At the end of this second stage, students put away the materials and take their science notebooks to the discussion area, as described below.

Stage Three: Shared Reflection

We have found that whole-group discussions about science are most productive when students, even in the intermediate grades, leave their desks and sit together in an area that is designated for class discussions. Then they easily can talk in pairs and work together as a large group. They also can see the class data tables, graphs, word bank, and other graphic organizers more clearly as the teacher models and engages students in creating them.

During this reflective-discussion stage, have one set of concrete materials in the discussion area so that students can see the materials while the class reflects about what happened during the investigation and how the observations and data support the explanations the students are beginning to construct. When students are developing new understanding, they need to make connections with the concrete materials so they can remember their experiences. After more experience, they can look at a visual replication instead, such as an illustration of the materials they have been using. With more experience and knowledge, they can move beyond the concrete materials and a picture, and understand a more abstract representation such as a diagram or a graphic organizer (for example, a flow map or Venn diagram).

This movement from concrete materials to visual representation to abstract organizers and thinking is a crucial element in teaching science and science writing. When students have trouble understanding a new concept, and then writing about it, it often is because they have spent too little time with the concrete materials or moved too quickly from communicating about the concrete experience to understanding that experience in a more generalized or abstract way. For example, in a unit about sound, students know from their experiences during their investigation that when they struck a short nail it made a high pitch. But they will not understand until they have had more concrete experiences that the shorter the nail is, the higher the pitch it will make. They also have not had enough experience to understand the more abstract principle: length affects both the pitch and vibration of objects. So, when students first talk and write about their experiences, they need to begin by describing what they actually have observed and experienced. Then, as they have more concrete experiences, they will be able to construct ideas and write about more abstract principles.

During this shared reflection stage, guide students by asking questions about their observations and data and how these help form answers to the question they have been investigating. Be sure to ask about data that are inconsistent with other test results as well as whether the data support the predictions they wrote before the investigation.

Also periodically, ask students to turn to the person next to them and talk about their thinking. All students—not just those who participate in whole-class discussions—need opportunities to talk about their thinking and to use scientific language. This, in turn, will help them develop scientific language skills they can use in their writing. (The role of this scientific discourse in developing science knowledge and scientific skills as well as writing skills is critical, but it is not the subject of this book.)

Sometime during this reflective discussion, you also can do the following:

- Add new words to the science word bank as students have a need to know them. Especially with English language learners, ask students to repeat words out loud with you as they see them. Hearing and seeing the words at the same time will help everyone learn the vocabulary.
- Repeat important words and language multiple times.
- Expect students to answer questions in complete sentences. This will improve both their oral and written expression.

- Model the scientific language and thinking the students need to learn. For example, when students make claims, ask them what evidence they have to support their statements. Model how to use the frame "I think _____ . I think this because _____ ." ("*I think* thin wire has more resistance than thick wire. *I think this because* when we used thin wire, the bulb was dimmer. When we used thick wire, the bulb was brighter.")
- Model how to construct class data tables and graphs, involving students in the process.
- Create graphic organizers if necessary (such as tables, T-charts, system-parts maps, and flow maps) to represent what students have been learning.

Chapters 3, 4, and 5 explain in greater detail when and how you introduce and model these components of the science and writing instruction.

By the end of this third stage, the reflective discussion, students usually have developed an understanding of the answer to the focus or investigative question. They also may have unresolved questions about the results of their investigations and additional questions to investigate.

Stage Four: Application

In the last stage of the teaching-learning sequence, guide students in thinking about how the information might apply to the real world or lead into another investigation or research through the Internet or books. Students might refer to their notebooks at this point to give them some ideas during the discussion, but they do not write during this last stage of the teaching-learning sequence of the science session.

In the Science Notebooks Program, we highly value the thinking and planning in which students engage during this stage. But, as mentioned in Chapter 1, because elementary school students have a restricted amount of time and energy to devote to science writing, we focus their writing on the thinking involved in the investigation they have conducted and discussed in the first three stages. They will not write in their notebooks again until they engage in a separate shared-writing minilesson and independent writing session, which is explained in the next section.

Science-Writing Session: Shared-Writing Minilesson and Independent Writing

This separate twenty- to thirty-minute writing session includes a review of the science session that preceded it, a minilesson about writing various forms of expository and scientific text, and independent writing time during which students make entries in their notebooks. You will need to schedule this block later in the day of the science lesson or some time the next day. If you wait longer than this, you will lose needed momentum in both the science and writing instruction.

Step One: Shared Review

You can begin this writing session (see Figure 2–3) by involving your students in a review of what they had concluded at the end of the shared reflection stage of the science session. Bring one set of concrete materials to the discussion area to help students remember what they have experienced. As the class reviews the end of the earlier discussion, do not provide a summary of the reflective discussion. Instead, ask questions, including the focus or investigative question, so that students are actively involved in the brief discussion.

Step Two: Shared Writing

After the shared review, explain to students that you are going to help them learn how to write in a certain way to communicate what they have learned. Then involve them in a shared-writing experience or minilesson in which you model writing certain phrases or writing structures—in other words, the *structure* of the writing—and students then contribute their observations, evidence, and thinking that constitutes the *content* of the writing. (Chapters 4 and 5 explain this process for different types of scientific writing.) The following example of a shared-writing minilesson can serve as an introduction to this process.

Writing Session: Shared-Writing Minilesson and Independent Writing				
Steps	**1. Shared Review**	**2. Shared Writing**	**3. Scaffolding**	**4. Independent Writing**
Teacher	Questions students about shared reflection of conclusions from previous science session.	Models structure of specific writing form (e.g., comparison, conclusion).	Writes scaffolding for notebook entry (e.g., sentence starters, phrases, words).	Works with small groups or individuals who need extra support or more challenges. Asks questions, models language, rereads writing with students.
Students	Provide reflections, explanations.	Provide content of the writing.		Use scaffolding as they write their own notebook entries.

FIGURE 2–3 Science-writing session

In *Circuits and Pathways*, a unit published by Insights, fourth graders investigate this question: What happens to the brightness of a bulb when you change the length of wire in a closed circuit? You can begin the shared writing by modeling a strategy for writing a conclusion to an investigative question, starting with a topic or opening sentence. First, discuss a *general* answer to the question. Students probably will say, "The brightness of the bulb changes." Then tell them that one way to begin a response is to use words from the question. If this is their first experience with this strategy, write a topic sentence on the overhead or board: "When you change the length of wire in a closed circuit, the brightness of the bulb changes." If students have used this strategy, you would ask for several examples rather than writing your own.

Next, tell students that they need to support this opening statement by providing evidence from their investigation (in other words, from their data tables or the class data table or graph). Write the words *For example*, and say that these words can introduce the supporting evidence or data. Teach them that when they provide evidence in a conclusion, they usually can *summarize* the evidence by providing data just from the lower or lowest and higher or highest ends of the range of data (not including outliers, or data that are inconsistent with the rest of the class data).

Now ask students to tell you the data from the lower or lowest end of the range shown in the class table or graph. Add the data to what you already have modeled: "For example, with 10 cm wire, the bulb brightness was 9." Before students provide the data from the other end of the range, model using a contrasting word such as *but* or *whereas* and add *only* to set up a contrast of the results: "*But* with the 30 cm wire, the bulb brightness was *only* 7."

Point out that they now have provided enough evidence to make a concluding statement, then model using *therefore* as one way to begin that statement. Finally, ask students to state their conclusion based on the data and add their words to yours: "Therefore, the longest wire makes the bulb dimmer and the shortest wire makes the bulb brighter."

If students have had enough experience with conducting controlled investigations with concrete materials and can recognize a cause-effect relationship between the length of wire and the brightness of a bulb, then ask them to write an inference about what is causing this difference. To model more structure, give them the phrase, "I think this is because." Students then might state something like, "I think this is because the longest wire has more resistance so the bulb is dimmer. The shortest wire has less resistance so the bulb shines more brightly."

Step Three: Scaffolding

Before students begin writing in their own science notebooks, remove the shared writing from the overhead or board. Replace it with just the scaffolding you have modeled during the shared writing. In the *Circuits* minilesson, the scaffolding is:

- Words from the question (topic sentence)
- "For example," (introduce data)
- "But" (introduce data from the other end of the range of data)
- "Therefore," (introduce concluding statement)
- "I think this because" (introduce inferential thinking)

Step Four: Independent Writing

Using the scaffolding (if they need to), students write a conclusion to their investigations in their notebooks. The scaffolding prompts them to include the components of a conclusion and also introduces them to a text structure that can help them write a conclusion.

This structured approach to teaching different forms of scientific writing works well with most students. Those who are learning English or have less developed language or writing skills benefit from having the scaffolding because it helps them learn the writing skills as well as how to think and write scientifically. Those with more advanced language skills benefit because they need to learn to write scientifically. And those who have highly developed language skills and rich background knowledge benefit from having to focus first on their evidence before leaping into their inferential thinking, which may or may not be accurate.

When students have learned how to provide evidence for their thinking, they do not need to use any scaffolding. Nor do they need to provide the evidence before their inferences unless, by explaining their inferential thinking first, they forget to write about their observations and measured data that substantiate their claims. Students do, however, need to include all these components, and often others as well, in their conclusions. Regardless of which text structures students are learning, be sure to ask them regularly, "What is another way we could write this?" Doing so will help students realize that the structure of any writing frame is not the only way to produce strong writing. It is only a place to begin. (See Chapters 4 and 5 for more information about shared-writing minilessons, specific forms of scientific writing, and ways to help students write fluently and independently.)

Audience for Science Notebook Entries

Throughout the years of the Science Notebooks Program, one of the most frequent feedback responses from the hundreds of teachers who have participated in the program addresses the issue of audience. With whom are the students communicating when they write their entries? The most common answer is the classroom teacher. But if a teacher is the audience, then students tend to try to do what they think will please their teacher. Students also assume then that the audience knows what students have done and discussed. This does not help students learn to write to an audience outside the classroom, which is an important writing skill. Furthermore, the standards for the notebook entries are often seen as those of the teacher.

What has worked extremely well in our program is to establish that other scientists are the audience. The standards of communication, therefore, are those of science. So, for example, when a student provides minimal information in an observation, you could ask, "What do you think another scientist would need to know if she or he were trying to understand more about what you observed?" Or say a student provides no evidence or only partial evidence for a claim. You might ask, "What do you think another scientist would need to know in order for you to convince him or her that your conclusion is reasonable?" After such queries, students can add information or reasoning to their entries.

Especially because we are thinking of students as young scientists who are communicating with adult scientists, talk with students about "making entries in their science notebooks." Many science programs refer to this process as "notebooking." But if we want students to think and act like scientists, we need to use appropriate language. Presumably, adult scientists do not say they are "notebooking" any more than they refer to their work as "sciencing."

Content of Science Notebooks in the Elementary Grades

Science programs vary in what they expect students to include in their science notebooks. To determine the content, you first have to determine your purpose in having students write in notebooks. As explained in Chapter 1, Seattle's Science Notebooks Program sees the notebooks as a means of teaching students to think scientifically and to learn expository writing structures that help them develop and communicate their scientific thinking and understanding. The program also advocates that teachers use the notebooks for formative rather than summative assessment and that they not score the notebooks. (Chapter 6 explains the rationale and research for this approach, how to assess the notebooks for formative assessment purposes, and how to communicate with students about their notebook entries.)

If you share this belief in the purpose of elementary science notebooks, then when you are deciding what type of entries students should make in their notebooks—in other words, the *content* of their notebooks—consider this fundamental question: How will writing these notebook entries help develop the students' *understanding of the science concepts and/or scientific skills and thinking*? Their writing experience should focus their attention and energy on learning to write about their observations and test results, as well as explain their thinking and conceptual understanding. The process of learning how to write, and then writing independently, in these ways actually will help students develop their scientific understanding and their thinking and scientific skills.

With this in mind, avoid having children write about how they felt about doing the investigation, what their favorite object or organism or lesson was, what they learned (as prompted by the generic question, What did you learn today?), and what they did. None of these prompts will encourage most students to think and write scientifically. For example, writing about materials and how they set up and conducted an investigation—in other words, what they *did*—will not help students develop understanding of scientific content. As noted earlier in this chapter, students should thoroughly *discuss* and write notes on a class or group chart about how they are going to set up and conduct an investigation because planning an investigation is an important scientific skill. But students do not need to write about all the components of an investigation. Elementary students are better served by concentrating on learning higher-level writing and thinking skills.

Many science-writing programs set up lists of requirements for the content of each notebook entry, which often are tied to a rubric system for assessing notebook entries. Because the Science Notebooks Program has a different emphasis and also does not promote using a rubric system for scoring elementary science notebooks, the content of each entry varies. What students write depends on what they need to be thinking about, as well as what kinds of writing they need to be learning in order to communicate that thinking. (Chapter 7 explains how to plan the writing for a science unit, including when to have students learn the different forms of scientific writing.) The only generic notebook requirements are that students should do the following:

1. Date, in numerals, the first page of the entry.
2. Write a focus or investigative question for each lesson.
3. Write something about each science session.
4. Write legibly (not necessarily their "best handwriting").

In this integrated science-writing approach, notebook entries are considered rough drafts. The writing process generally has four stages: prewriting, rough draft, editing or revision, and publishing. In the prewriting stage of a science notebook entry, students engage in discussions and create organizers (for example, class tables, T-charts, and graphs) to help them think about and organize what they will write (as explained in Chapters 4 and 5). They also participate in a shared-writing minilesson and independent writing session (as explained earlier in this chapter). In the rough draft phase of writing, students focus on the following three traits:

1. *content*, which addresses scientific content or conceptual understanding;
2. *organization*, which includes scientific thinking and the structure of different types of scientific writing (for example, observations, comparisons, and conclusions); and
3. *word choice*, which includes accurate use of scientific vocabulary.

If teachers or students choose to take an entry through the entire writing process—publishing an entry as a scientific article, for example—then students edit and revise the entry in terms of three other writing traits: sentence fluency (the flow of the language and variety of sentence structures), voice (a sense of scientific authority that a student expresses through the writing), and conventions (spelling, punctuation, and grammar). The point here is not that these last three traits are unimportant. However, at certain stages in the writing, and thinking, process, we need to focus students' attention on certain traits. This also helps many reluctant writers learn to enjoy writing because they are so engaged in scientific work and thinking that is meaningful to them.

Neatness, handwriting, and presentation also would be important in a published piece. In a rough draft, however, the writing needs only to be *legible* to other readers. For example, if you teach students in the intermediate grades, allow them to choose whether they want to print or write their entries in cursive so they are not restricted by the handwriting itself.

Teachers in our science-writing program, especially in the primary grades, have difficulty letting go of the idea that the notebooks should be a product that looks good. However, as teachers learn to focus on developing students' scientific thinking and teaching expository text structures that communicate higher-level science understanding, they change their assessment focus and concentrate on the *content* of the writing. (Chapter 6 includes information about how to assess student notebook entries through this lens.)

Physical Characteristics of Science Notebooks

What you choose to use for science notebooks is going to depend on the resources you have in your school or district. But here are some guidelines based on what we have tested and found to be most effective.

Size

Notebooks that are eight and one-half by eleven inches provide the best space. For example, when students need to compare two organisms, the larger paper allows them to draw and write an observation on a left-hand page, then draw and write about the other organism on the facing right-hand page. Having the illustrations on facing pages makes it easier for students to set up a comparison of the two (as explained in Chapter 4).

Students also can write more effectively about data when a table or graph is on a left-hand page and students write their analysis on the facing right-hand page (see Chapter 5 for writing about data). Keeping ongoing records of observations—of a plant, for instance—often requires using a table that is eleven by seventeen inches. This, too, enables students to see in one place the data they have collected over time (as explained in Chapter

4). Students tape such a table to a notebook page before folding the table into the notebook, so the notebook has to be eleven inches on the side.

Lined Pages

Except for kindergartners, who use unlined pages, students need to write on lined notebook pages. Some teachers in primary grades like to have paper that is partly unlined and partly lined. In our experience, these types of pages restrict both the quality and quantity of the student writing. So does paper that is designed for handwriting instruction. Students should not be worrying about their handwriting when they are making thoughtful entries in their notebooks. The requirement is that notebook entries are legible. Consequently, teachers do not mention handwriting in discussing or assessing the notebooks unless a student is careless and has written illegible text.

Binding

The notebook pages should be bound in some way rather than loose because the science notebook represents an ongoing record of a student's observations, data, thinking, and developing understanding. Sewn bindings work best, but spiral-bound notebooks work well, too, because they keep the pages organized and intact, and are sturdy enough to survive rough treatment.

Science "Notebooks"

We refer to these notebooks as *science notebooks* to distinguish them, in both teachers' and students' minds, from journals or logs. *Journals* often are associated with process writing and writing workshops in which students choose what they want to write and approach their writing in a particular way. *Science logs* tend to be ongoing records of the process of science, including questions, hypotheses, materials, procedures, and claims based on test results.

Using *science notebooks* in this science-writing program integrates the processes of learning how to think and write about science. Students do not choose, as they do with writing journals, the subject of an entry, and they learn disciplined forms of scientific writing through highly structured instruction. In addition, students do not record every aspect of their investigations in their notebooks, as they would in science logs, so that other scientists can replicate their experiments. Instead, these notebooks are meant to serve a different purpose: to focus student thinking and writing on targeted components of scientific investigations and scientific thinking in order to maximize the learning of scientific concepts, skills, thinking, and writing.

Important Points to Remember

1. Plan to have a science session and a science-writing session for each lesson in your science unit.
2. Model scientific skills, thinking, and language orally and in writing.
3. Help students recognize what an audience of adult scientists would expect and need to see in science notebook entries.
4. Understand that science notebooks are rough drafts, so students should focus on the following when they are writing their entries:
   - Content (science concepts and thinking)
   - Organization (scientific thinking and skills)
   - Word choice (scientific vocabulary and clarity of word use)
   - Legibility (readable; not necessarily good handwriting)

CHAPTER THREE

Developing and Organizing Scientific Understanding and Thinking

Science Word Banks and Graphic Organizers

As students begin to develop their scientific thinking and understanding through scientific inquiry, they need structures that help them organize their thinking, remember what they are learning, and deepen their understanding. The process of making and using graphic organizers such as science word banks, tables, system-parts maps, and diagrams becomes part of their learning. Students then use these as prewriting structures that help them write thoughtful, detailed, organized notebook entries.

We use graphic organizers extensively in the Science Notebooks Program. This chapter explains why and how we use them to give students the visual support they need as they develop new skills and understanding. Students also will create their own tables and other organizers in their notebooks, as described in Chapters 4 and 5.

Science Word Banks

One of the fundamental components of both our science and science-writing programs is the science word bank. Figure 3–1 shows a word bank in a fifth-grade classroom. Instead of writing words on a chart or the board, you make word cards and place them, when appropriate, in a pocket chart. This allows you to pick up the cards and show them to your students so they can hear and see the new vocabulary as they learn to use the words in their scientific investigations and thinking.

The cards also are useful in modeling scientific skills. For example, you can take the words out of the word bank and have students sort and classify

FIGURE 3–1 Word bank in a fifth-grade classroom

them, which will help students see relationships among the words, a higher-level thinking skill. You also can use the cards to show explicit connections among the words, their meanings, and their spelling (for example, the word *quantitative* has the same root as *quantity* and refers to measured data). Because the words are mobile, you can hold them up during class discussions when you want to reinforce the meaning or usage of certain words.

When and How to Add Words to the Word Bank

Place a word card in the science word bank after students have had a concrete experience with something and have a need to know the appropriate term. Imagine, for example, that a second-grade class has been working with a balance beam resting on a wooden block to explore the concept of balance. During small-group and whole-class discussions, students keep referring to the "wooden block." At this point, the teacher can tell them that scientists (or physicists) call the block the *fulcrum* or *pivot point*. In this way, students can connect their concrete experience with terms that previously would have been abstract and meaningless to them.

This is a caveat in inquiry-based science: Students must learn scientific vocabulary *after* they have had a *concrete experience*. As stated in *How Students Learn*, published by the National Research Council of the National Academies: "Ideas develop from experiences, and technical terms develop from the ideas and operations that are rooted in those experiences. When terms come first, students just tend to memorize so much technical jargon that it sloughs off in a short while" (Donovan and Bransford 2005, 512).

Before you place a newly introduced word in the word bank, read the word together so students focus on the sounds and spelling of the word. Then when you place the card in the pocket chart, organize the words conceptually, rather than randomly or alphabetically, as you add them. For instance, in *Land and Water*, a fourth-grade earth science unit by Science and Technology for Children (STC), the term *soil* might be grouped with the words *humus*, *clay*, and *sand* (as shown in Figure 3–1). The term *water flow* might be grouped with *slope* and *gravity*. Visually and conceptually, then, the terms are closely linked, which will help students learn the new vocabulary more easily.

As students progress through a unit of study, you and the class may need to reorganize the words so that they are grouped according to how the unit is evolving conceptually. In some cases, this may happen with each lesson. This type of organization helps students see relationships among terms and concepts, and helps children find the words they need to use in their writing. Because this vocabulary development is so critical in developing scientific thinking and understanding, especially with ELL students who are learning English, you and the students will use the science word bank throughout each science unit.

When planning each science session or lesson, anticipate science terms and other important words that students may need to use in their writing, and prepare word cards ahead of time. Also have blank word cards handy for words that you think of during the session and words that students suggest. Even when their words are not scientific, including them helps students transition from their vocabulary to the more sophisticated terms.

Generic Science Vocabulary

In addition to learning words that are unit specific, students also need to develop generic science vocabulary, which you can add as needed to a separate part of the science word bank or just outside the pocket chart if the unit vocabulary is filling the word bank. The generic terminology includes both terms and phrases, and varies in form depending on whether the students are in primary or intermediate grades. In primary grades, the cards might include such phrases as *I predict, I observed,* and *I noticed* as well as *because, evidence,* and *fair test.* Intermediate grades might include more sophisticated terms such as *predict/prediction, observe/observation, investigate/investigation, infer/inference, controlled investigation,* and *variable.*

Continue to add terms and phrases as needed, just as you do with the unit-specific vocabulary. Writing the generic words in a color that is different from the one you use for the unit vocabulary helps distinguish the two sets of words. The last two rows of word cards in the word bank shown in Figure 3–1 are generic words, so they are grouped together and written in a different color than the unit words. You can reuse the generic word cards with every science unit.

Using Icons and Other Visual Aids on Word Cards

In some cases, you may need to add an icon or simple diagram to a word card to help students remember the term's meaning. Figure 3–2 shows a second-grade teacher using word cards with icons to remind his students about the meaning and symbols they are using for *heavier than* and *lighter than* in STC's *Balancing and Weighing* unit.

In the intermediate grades, the vocabulary becomes even more complex. For instance, when fourth graders first are learning about electric circuits, they know from their experiences how they must set up a circuit in order to make a bulb light up. However, they may have trouble remembering specific terms: a circuit is *complete* or *closed* when the bulb turns on and is *open* when the bulb does not turn on. The word card for *open circuit*, then, could include an icon representing an incomplete circle and the card for *complete* or *closed circuit* could show a complete circle. Some children, such as ELL students, might need more detailed support such as a simple diagram of a circuit with the bulb lit up (with lines radiating from the bulb) or a circuit with an unlit bulb.

In other instances, all students may need more concrete reminders of new vocabulary. For example, in *Rocks and Minerals*, a third-grade earth science unit published by STC, students conduct light tests to determine whether each mineral is opaque, translucent, or transparent. Before conducting the tests, you can have students shine a light on tag board, waxed paper, and plastic wrap in order to see approximations of how the light tests will work with minerals. After this concrete experience, you can introduce the three terms. Write the terms on word cards, then attach a piece of

FIGURE 3–2 Teacher uses word cards with icons

tag board to the card for *opaque*, waxed paper to *translucent*, and plastic wrap to *transparent*. Connecting their concrete experiences with the new vocabulary will help students learn the terms. Having the vocabulary connected with the concrete associations in the science word bank will help students remember the words as well as the spelling.

Kindergartners need even more visual and concrete supports than older students do. In the word banks for typical kindergarten units such as *Wood* and *Fabric*, published by Full Option Science System (FOSS), you can place an example of each type of wood or fabric next to its identifying word card. Adding a couple of descriptive words next to the piece of wood or fabric (for example, *fleece—soft, thick*) also helps build students' vocabulary and spelling skills.

More concrete support is needed for more sophisticated vocabulary. For instance, before having students explore how some wood and fabrics absorb or repel water, students first can use pipettes to drop water on pieces of paper towel and waxed paper. Then you can show them word cards that illustrate different word usage. On one word card, you can write *absorbs water* and attach a piece of paper towel; on a second card, you can write *repels water* and attach waxed paper. Because the words *repel* and *absorb* apply to what the fabric and wood do with the water but do not describe what the water does, you will need to make two more cards. On the third card, you can write *water beads up* and make an icon of a straight line with half of a sphere above it, then attach a piece of waxed paper. On a fourth card, you can write *water soaks in* and make a straight line with shading below it, then attach a piece of paper towel. This not only reinforces vocabulary development, but also models how students can make simple diagrams to communicate results of their investigations.

Making Word Cards Accessible for Young Students

In kindergarten and early first grade, many teachers also make multiple smaller copies of the word cards and place them next to cards in the word bank. When it is time for students to write in their science notebooks, they come up to the word bank and take words back to their desks. This increases their ability to write independently.

Other primary-grade teachers choose to make multiple small word cards for each lesson, which they then distribute in individual envelopes to each table group of students when it is time for them to write in their science notebooks. Having the words right at their desks makes the vocabulary even more accessible for young students. Teachers store these cards in envelopes for each lesson and use them year after year, adding new words when necessary.

Labeled Illustrations as Word Banks in Life Science

In life science, where students need to learn the parts and functions of life systems, creating an enlarged scientific illustration as a class after students have observed an organism works as a "graphic science word bank." Seeing and learning words posted in a pocket chart, in this case, is not as effective as seeing terms right next to a part in an illustration of an organism. If students have observed a goldfish, for example, you can model drawing an enlarged scientific illustration on chart paper (see Figure 3–3). As you ask students what they observed in each area of the body, model how to draw the parts. Then you can discuss the name and the function of each part, labeling all the parts in one color and all the functions in another color. This color-coding emphasizes that each part has a function. And because the illustration is part of the classroom environment, students will be able to refer to it during class discussions and independent writing, which will reinforce both conceptual and vocabulary development. (See Chapter 4 for more information about teaching students how to make observations and scientific illustrations.)

What to Do When the Science Word Bank Is Full

In many units, you will run out of space in the word bank as the unit progresses. As that begins to happen, move the generic words to another area near the word bank. If you still need more space, check to see if all the vocabulary is still pertinent. Some words are critical at first, but become less so in later lessons. Depending on the situation, you can place the cards behind other cards in the word bank, or place them outside the word bank so students still can see them.

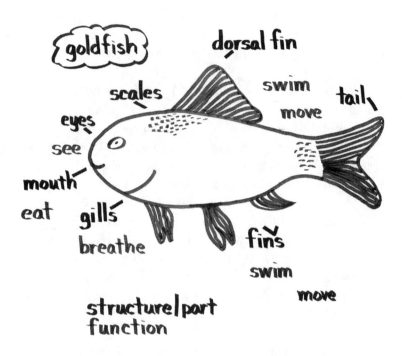

FIGURE 3–3 Enlarged scientific illustration

Placement of Science Word Banks

To facilitate and maximize the use of the science word bank, put it in a place that is clearly designated for science. Ideally, you also would have word banks for other content areas such as mathematics and social studies because this support is so important for vocabulary development, especially for students who are learning English. Each of these word banks also would have its own area so that students always know where to look to retrieve vocabulary for discussions and writing.

In kindergarten and first-grade classrooms, hang the pocket chart low enough so that students easily can read and have access to the word cards. Remember, too, that you want all students to be able to see the words from their desks as they are writing, so make the words large and bold by using dark-colored and fairly broad-tipped markers.

Graphic Organizers

Graphic organizers provide critical visual support as students are developing skills and conceptual understanding. In science, the organizers typically take the form of tables, T-charts, system-parts maps, flow maps, concept maps, and graphs. (Figure 3–4 shows some typical graphic organizers.) Science word banks and other means of organizing information in visual displays are important as well. The key idea here is that students are learning new ways of thinking and new concepts; they need visual

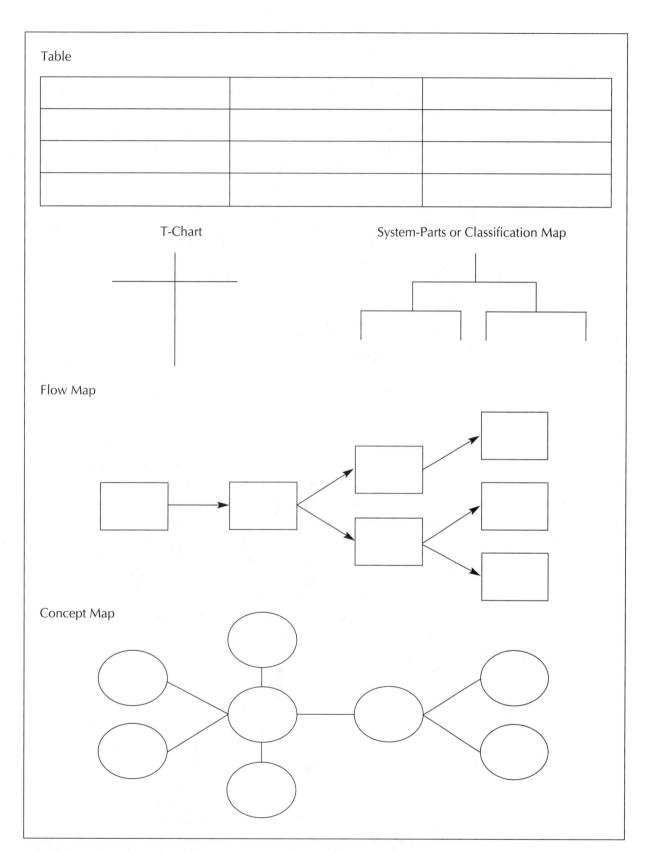

FIGURE 3–4 Examples of graphic organizers

representations of various kinds to help them learn and remember this new knowledge.

As much as possible, students should take part in some way during class discussions in developing these organizers so that they experience how to take disorganized data and ideas and arrange them in an organized visual or graphic way. This process helps students learn how to organize their thinking, which often leads to deeper understanding.

Generally, students do not copy these organizers into their notebooks. However, in some cases, students will have copies of generic organizers, such as for making observations or planning an investigation, at their desks. In other cases, when the organizer is being constructed to represent a new concept or to compile data from group investigations, then you would model how to make an organizer such as a system-parts map or a table, engaging students in the process by asking for their input. Then students use their own data or observations to create organizers in their notebooks. (Chapters 4 and 5 explain more about how to use organizers and writing frames in helping students make different types of entries in their notebooks and learn different forms of scientific writing.)

Using Graphic Organizers to Teach Scientific Skills

In helping students develop scientific skills and thinking, do not, as a general rule, use blackline masters provided in the unit teacher's guide. With teacher modeling and ongoing practice, students can create their own illustrations, diagrams, tables, and graphs in their notebook. The entries do not look as good as the professional versions, but students learn valuable scientific skills when they create their own entries. They also do much more writing than they are able to do on blackline masters.

Occasionally, especially in the primary grades, a table or graph might be too difficult or time-consuming for children to create. In such cases, have students fill out the blackline master, but add a meaningful question for them to write about as well. Some teacher's guides provide excellent questions to ask during each phase of a lesson. Questions from the reflection phase at the end of a lesson often are good prompts for student thinking and written responses in their notebooks. (Chapters 4 and 5 provide suggestions for teaching students how to make their own scientific illustrations, diagrams, tables, and graphs.)

Teachers can use certain graphic organizers to help students develop particular scientific skills. For example, students need to learn how to make detailed, accurate observations, but they often approach such a task quite randomly and ineffectively. While open exploration is critical to good inquiry experiences, students also benefit from following some guidelines as they get more involved in their investigation. The Observations organizer shown in Figure 3–5 hangs on the classroom wall, and helps you guide your classroom discussions of what students have observed. (These guidelines are generic, so you and your students will need to change them

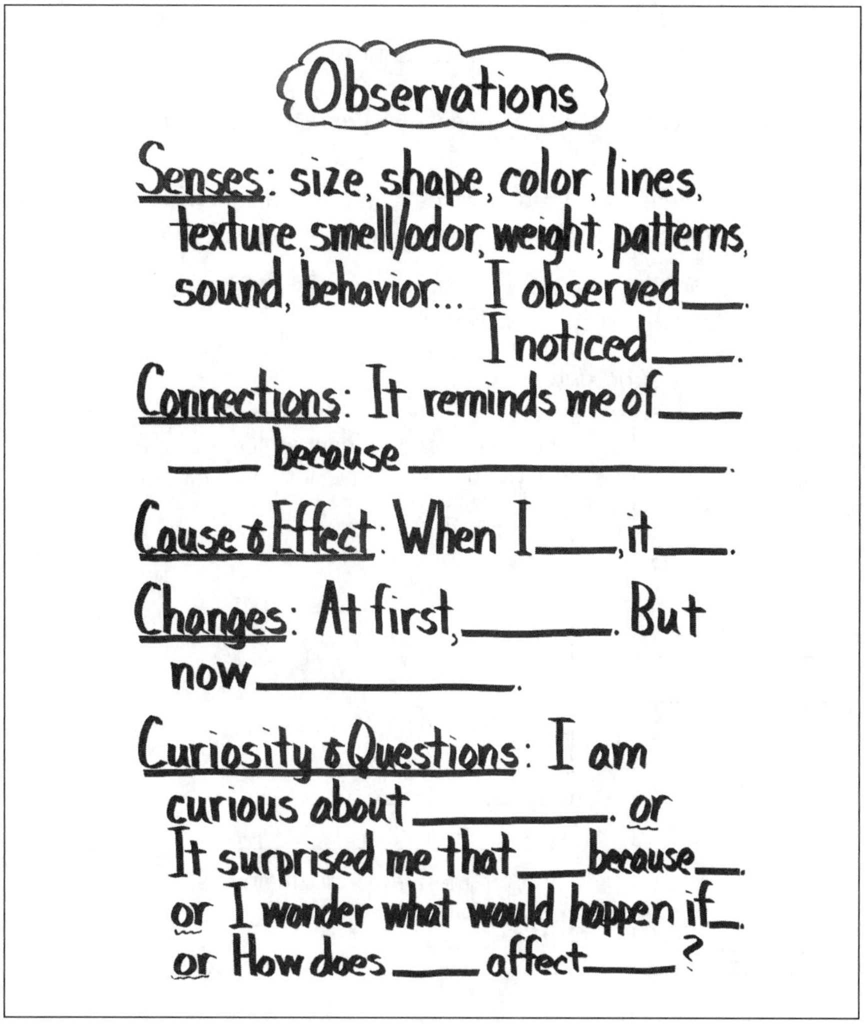

FIGURE 3–5 Classroom Observations organizer

as needed for your particular science unit.) While students are observing objects, organisms, or events, they can use a blackline master of this organizer to guide their observations. (Chapter 4 includes a detailed explanation of how to teach students to use the organizer. Appendix A includes the blackline master.) But it is important to have this enlarged copy in the classroom so everyone can refer to it during discussions.

Students also need to learn the scientific skills involved in planning a scientific investigation. Planning Your Own Scientific Investigation (see Figure 3–6) is an example of a detailed organizer that serves as a template to support intermediate students as they learn to plan a controlled investigation, as mentioned in Chapter 2. (The large classroom version for planning investigations is shown in that chapter.) Students can use this organizer to remind themselves of the essential components they must consider when planning, and making conclusions about, an investigation. It also includes important vocabulary they need to understand. (Seattle's Science

Planning Your Own Scientific Investigation

Use this form when you want to design and conduct your own investigation of a question that you and your group want to explore.

Investigative question (the question you want to investigate). Include both the changed (manipulated) variable and the measured/observed (responding) variable.

Prediction, including your reasoning. (You might write, *I predict* _____ *because* _____ .) Include the variable you will change and what you will measure/observe.

Procedure

List the one changed (manipulated) variable:	List the most important logical steps; include all the different variables and their amounts:
List the variables you will keep the same or constant (controlled variables):	
	List the most important materials:

List the variable you will measure and/or observe (measured/observed or responding variable):

How often and/or how many times will you measure and/or observe it?

Make a table for recording the data.
Repeat the tests/procedure at least 3 times.

After you have completed the investigation and talked with your group about the results, *write a conclusion*. Answer the *question that you have been investigating*, providing the data (results of your investigation) as *evidence of your thinking*. Also write about whether or not the results of the investigation support your *prediction*. If necessary, you might also explain what you think caused *inconclusive or inconsistent data* in your results (consider the *variables* in your tests).

FIGURE 3–6 Template for planning an investigation

Notebooks Program developed this template to help intermediate students learn the vocabulary and structure of inquiry investigations that fifth graders are expected to know on the state's science assessment.) In this integrated science-writing approach, students usually do not write up their investigation plan, but they benefit from using this type of organizer. It presents all the components of an investigation in a clear, visual way so that students can begin to learn about the different variables they need to consider in their planning. Students do not fill in the template. It serves more as a visual planning checklist of things to consider.

Making Organizers That Summarize Data and Conceptual Development

In many published units, students construct their understanding of certain subconcepts in a unit through conducting a series of investigations. For example, in *Sound*, an intermediate unit published by STC, students explore the relationship between the length of an object and its pitch by working with tuning forks, nails, and then rulers. By the end of three lessons, students have discovered the relationship between length and pitch.

To help the class represent and remember what they have learned, it is useful to help them create a class chart that summarizes the results of the investigations (see Figure 3–7). In making the chart, the teacher walks students through the process of constructing a chart or table—determining the title and the content of the columns and rows—with the students providing the necessary information while the teacher models how to make the chart. (Generally, *tables* have rows and columns and include data; *charts* typically have rows and columns, too, but include information rather than the data collected in investigations.) Because students have investigated only the variable of length, the class would make only that part of their chart. Then, after several more lessons in which they explore the variable of tension, they will have enough understanding to add a row about the effect of tension, and so on. The icons in the chart help students remember what the terms mean and also help them learn how to make diagrams that communicate information and understanding, which is a particularly useful skill in physical science.

Creating Complex Organizers

System-parts maps are useful when students need to see the various components of a system and how they relate to one another. In life science units in which fourth and fifth graders study complex ecosystems, for instance, it is helpful for students to learn how to make such an organizer so they easily can see all the living and nonliving parts, as shown in Figure 3–8. (Primary students benefit from using much simpler system-parts maps of the habitats that they create.) In this complex case, students might want to make this organizer in their notebooks—after they have created it as a

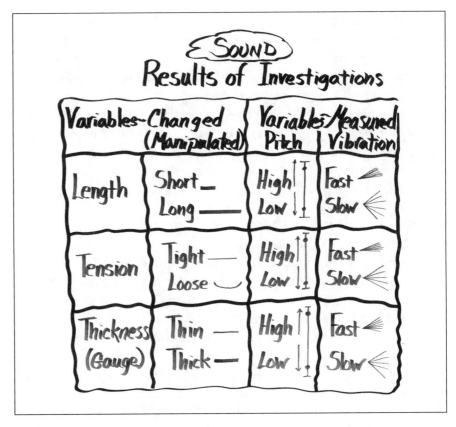

FIGURE 3–7 Results of Investigations chart

class—so they can easily use the details of the graphic to remind them of all the parts of the system. This also will help them write detailed, organized descriptions of what they observe in the aquarium over time.

In addition, in studying ecosystems, students often need to learn how to create graphic representations of relationships within systems, such as interdependencies and dependencies (as shown at the bottom of Figure 3–8). This is a complicated concept, and the process of creating the organizer together, then writing it in the science notebooks, can help students become more familiar with the concepts.

Some teachers like to construct concept maps of ecosystems and the concepts of interdependence and dependence. But these organizers become confusing visual representations, not only as references for discussions throughout the unit but also as prewriting structures. Figure 3–9 shows such a concept map that a teacher drew on the overhead. Compare it with the organizers shown in Figure 3–8 and imagine how students would use each of the organizers. In creating visual supports for your students, always anticipate where students might get confused and help them learn to create the clearest possible organizers. This ultimately will be a useful skill as they encounter more complex and abstract concepts after elementary school.

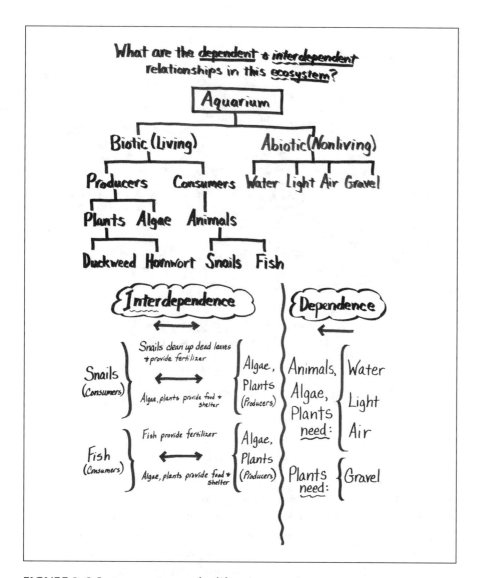

FIGURE 3–8 System-parts map for life science unit

Placement of Graphic Organizers

Because every content area (science, mathematics, and social studies, for example) and the skills-based domains of reading and writing need to have visual supports for learning, adequate space can be an issue. Consequently, you might want to take a visual inventory of your classroom. To be useful, science word banks, graphic organizers, and other visual aids for students must stand out or students will tune them out. Are there posters or other things on your classroom walls that are not essential to learning? While it is important to create a warm atmosphere, we often include too many unnecessary things on our valuable board and wall space.

On the other hand, we also need to be careful not to overwhelm students with too many organizers and other supports for learning. To maintain a balance, consider using flip-charts for displaying organizers and

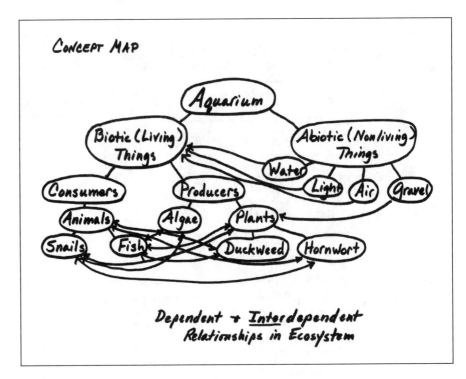

FIGURE 3–9 Ineffective use of graphic organizer

other visuals you do not need on an ongoing basis. Depending on your classroom, you might be able to display generic organizers (for example, observations guidelines) above your chalkboard or white board. In open-concept classrooms that do not have walls, you can construct charts and other organizers from tag board, then hang them from clotheslines.

Figure 3–10 shows the science area of a second-grade classroom. Students are studying *Balancing and Weighing,* a primary unit published by STC. Note that the words in the science word bank on the left are organized by how they relate to each other in terms of the concepts of balancing and weighing. The next graphic organizer is a box and T-chart, which students use in making comparisons (the strategy is described in Chapter 4). Next is a class data table that includes quantitative (measured) data that pairs of students have collected in their investigations. The teacher fills in data tables during class discussions about the results of their investigations. The last organizer is a class data table for collecting students' notes about their observations (qualitative data). Also note the word cards *solid* and *hollow.* The teacher has just introduced these terms during the reflective class discussion. He will place them in the science word bank later on.

In addition to referring to the class graphic organizers during discussions and in shared-writing minilessons, students will use some class organizers as they write in their science notebook during the writing session. For example, if each group of students has added test results to a class data table or a graph, as shown in Figure 3–10, then the students might refer to

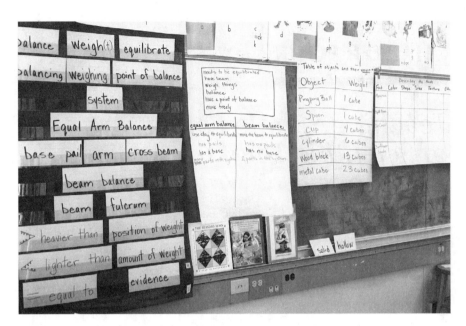

FIGURE 3–10 Science area in a second-grade classroom

that table or graph as they write about the class data. On the other hand, if student groups have been doing their own investigations, such as growing plants in certain conditions, they might discuss results from all the groups, but then write using data from their own tables in their notebooks. In any case, using graphic organizers will help them write detailed, organized, and accurate entries that also will include appropriate vocabulary because of the science word bank.

Three Important Requirements

The most important requirements to remember in creating and using science word banks and other visual organizers effectively are:

1. Students must be able to see the class organizers easily and clearly.
2. The organizers must be well organized and supportive of the students' learning.
3. Teachers must use them regularly in discussions during science sessions and in modeling during writing sessions.

Chapters 4 and 5 will explain more about how students can use graphic organizers as they actually write different types of entries in their science notebooks.

Reference

Donovan, M. S., and J. D. Bransford, eds. 2005. *How Students Learn: Science in the Classroom*. Washington, DC: The National Academies Press.

CHAPTER FOUR

Teaching Simple Forms of Scientific Thinking and Expository Writing

Observations, Cause and Effect, and Comparisons

Elementary students understand how to write a story because the structure is familiar and linear, with a beginning, a middle, and an end. But with the exception of procedural writing and chronological reporting, scientific writing is not linear. Observation, cause and effect, comparison, data summary and interpretation, reasoning, and conclusion all have primarily nonlinear structures. They are organized by sequences of logic rather than of time.

Because your students are not familiar with this analytical way of thinking, talking, and writing, you need to model both the oral and written language as you guide students in developing their scientific thinking and understanding. Using such language in class discussions helps students learn the vocabulary and develop "an ear" for the structure and components of scientific language. In shared-writing minilessons (at a separate time from the science session, as noted in Chapter 2), you can model how to write in these different forms. These are "shared" experiences because students provide the *content* of the writing while you model the *structure* and *language* to communicate that content. Students then write in their science notebooks, guided at first by sentence starters and writing frames that you give them, as well as useful words and phrases posted on class charts and in the science word bank. The ultimate goal is for students to learn the language and the structures so they can write responses independently.

Many teachers in the Science Notebooks Program initially report that their students struggle when they must transition from talking about their scientific thinking to writing about it. But most of the teachers discover that they can rectify the problem if they make two adjustments:

1. Schedule time during the science session to have deeper, more reflective class discussions in which they explicitly model scientific thinking and language.
2. Plan a separate writing session in which their students can actively participate in a shared-writing minilesson in which they learn how to structure a particular entry.

Such instruction requires additional scheduling, but these teachers find that the results are worth the time, especially as their students' thinking and writing improve in other content areas as well as in science.

Before these discussions and minilessons, your students must engage in meaningful, concrete experiences in which they can begin to construct conceptual understanding and develop scientific skills. As they begin to explore, they need to learn how to make careful, thorough observations, which is not something that most students do naturally. They also must learn how to recognize and describe causal relationships and to make strong comparisons. This chapter focuses on strategies that teach children how to make careful, thoughtful observations and comparisons and then write about them in their science notebooks. (Chapter 5 addresses more complex writing about reasoning, data, and conclusions.)

Making Detailed Observations

To write good observations, students first must learn how to observe carefully, using all their senses except taste. Then they learn to record detailed, organized observations in scientific illustrations, diagrams, and/or notes.

Guiding Observations

To guide children in making detailed observations, you and the students can use the generic Observations organizer in Figure 4–1, which was introduced in Chapter 3 as a graphic organizer you can display in your classroom. Students use a copy of this organizer, which they can keep in their science notebook, while they are making their observations. (The blackline master is included in Appendix A.) During class reflective discussions, everyone refers to the enlarged version on the wall. Because this is a generic organizer, you and the class will need to adapt this version to your unit of study. Over time, students will learn how to make observations without such support.

As students use the organizer, they focus on details they might not otherwise notice. For example, asking children to respond to the question "What do you see?" typically results in very general responses. "What does it look like?" generally prompts students to make vague or irrelevant analogies.

Observations	
Think of the four senses (not taste).	Size, shape, color, lines, patterns, texture, weight, smell/odor, sound, behavior . . .
	I observed _____ .
	I noticed _____ .
Connect it with what you know or have investigated.	It reminds me of _____ because _____ .
Observe and record cause and effect.	When _____ , it _____ .
Note any changes.	At first, _____ . But now _____ .
Be curious, and ask questions you might investigate.	I am curious about _____ . It surprised me that _____ because _____ .
	I wonder what would happen if _____ .
	How does _____ affect _____ ?

FIGURE 4–1 Observations organizer

But if you ask, "What did you notice about the color?" (or the size, shape, texture, patterns, and so on), then students not only will notice and articulate more of what they have observed, but they also will begin to recognize the kinds of characteristics or properties they should be considering. At this point, they also should begin verbalizing such phrases as "I observed" and "I noticed," which they later will use in their writing.

To make connections with other knowledge, students should consider, at some point, the question "What does this remind me of?" This relational thinking has two levels. At the beginning of a unit, their thinking may be based only on prior personal knowledge rather than scientific experience. So, for example, if a young child is asked, "What does [the soil component] humus remind you of?" he might mention the dirt in his grandmother's garden. Initially, this is an important connection, but after the student has explored the properties of soil during a scientific unit of study, then you would expect him to refer back to previous investigations. He might say, for instance, that the way the local soil settles in the water reminds him of how the humus settled in a previous settling test. This is important higher-level thinking, which the question has prompted.

Describing Cause and Effect, and Changes Over Time

Another component of effective observations involves cause and effect, prompted by a question such as "What happens when you . . . ?" For example, in a life science unit, you might ask, "What happens when you touch the pillbug?" In the class discussion, you would model speaking and, later, writing the words "When I . . . " to begin the observation. Then in the writing minilesson, you would model how to begin a sentence with the introductory clause "When I . . . ." Students then will learn how to increase the fluency of their writing by using such clauses while also communicating their understanding of causal relationships.

Christine, a kindergartner, wrote the entry in Figure 4–2. She is served in the English Language Learner (ELL) Program, as are about 60 percent of the students in her school. In the fall, she knew only the names of letters. Throughout the year, her teacher has been integrating this science-writing approach with her inquiry-based science instruction. Outside of science, she uses similar strategies such as oral modeling of language and labeled visual representations of objects and ideas to increase language development.

FIGURE 4–2 Christine's observation entry

Christine's notebook entry is from the kindergartners' third science unit, *Animals Two by Two* (published by Full Option Science System or FOSS), so she knows how to make a scientific illustration as she observes the animal. She adds labels for the parts and their functions as the class discusses their observations and the teacher adds labels to her drawing on the overhead. Christine adds her own label for the mucous trail, which she had seen and felt, then adds *move* to indicate that the mucous helps the snail move. To write a response to the second focus question about behavior, she uses inventive spelling and words from cards her teacher has written (which also are in the science word bank) and given to each table group for that lesson: "When I tuch [touch] the snail's tentacle it suks [sucks] in the body." She has learned the cause-and-effect structure "When I" in discussions during science and in writing sessions.

A more complex version of this modeling is typical in an intermediate unit such as *Sound*, published by Science and Technology for Children (STC). In a class discussion about an investigation in which students pluck strings of different lengths to determine their pitches, students can learn to use introductory clauses as well as comparative language in their speaking and writing. Using the concrete materials the students have been using, you can model how to talk—and later write—about their test results: "When I plucked the *short* string, it made a *high* pitch. *But* when I plucked the *long* string, it made a *low* pitch." Then, to increase the complexity, introduce the superlative comparisons: "When I plucked the *shortest* string, it made the *highest* pitch. When I plucked the *longest* string, it made the *lowest* pitch." During the writing minilesson, you can model the same language as you conduct a shared-writing minilesson. If students use their table of recorded observations or data as a checklist or organizer, they will remember to report the results for the shortest and longest strings.

This verbal and written modeling is extremely helpful for ELL and special education students because it provides scaffolding for the language that communicates specific kinds of experiences or thinking. It also benefits students who have good language skills but who need help in providing details and organizing their writing and thinking.

Students also need to be able to observe and describe changes over time (for example, how a plant or animal changes during its life cycle). These changes can be described as a kind of contrast. Writing about observations of such change over time is described in the "Comparisons" section later in this chapter. A conclusion about changes caused by pollution, which has a similar structure but involves higher-level thinking and writing, is discussed in the description of Figure 5–20 in Chapter 5.

Focusing and Organizing Observations

During some observations, students need to focus their attention on certain parts or areas of what they are observing in order to describe and write about them accurately and clearly. For example, in *Land and Water*, a unit published for fourth graders by STC, students use a stream table as a model of a stream system (see Figure 4–3). Often, when teachers ask students to describe what they see in the stream table, the students' responses are incomplete and disorganized, in part because children skip around and leave things out. One way to solve this problem is to place two strings across the stream table, dividing it into three parts. Then you can guide the observation by asking them to focus on and discuss what they notice in each area.

FIGURE 4–3 Students' stream table divided by strings

Ask them first what they notice at the beginning of the stream table. (Later in the unit, they will refer to this area as the *head* of the stream.) Next, ask them to describe what they see in the middle (later known as the *stream channel*). And finally, ask what they observe at the end (*mouth* and *delta*). In this way, the observation process is focused and scaffolded so that students can make detailed, organized observations.

During the shared reflection discussion (the third stage of the teaching-learning sequence explained in Chapter 2), model the transitional words that can frame this type of observation (for example, "At the beginning, ... Next, ... Finally, ..."). This will help students transfer the details of their stream-table observation into a scaffolding they can use in their writing. In this way, the stream table becomes both the visual organizer for the students' observations (beginning, middle, and end of the stream table) and the prewriting structure ("At the beginning, ... Next, ... Finally, ...") they can use in their writing.

The entry in Figure 4–4 is from the notebook of a fifth-grade boy named Jayred. He has strong science and math interests and skills, and receives special education services for reading and writing. Understandably, he writes reluctantly but is knowledgeable about the scientific investigations. Because of rich class discussions, teacher modeling, and practice using the stream table as an organizer, Jayred independently writes a strong description that is organized, accurate, clear, and rich in content vocabulary. This vocabulary is in the class science word bank, which he either uses as he writes this entry or has already used to help him learn how to spell the words. (Interestingly, *dirt*, which is one of the few words he misspells, is not in the word bank because *soil* is the scientific term.) His observation also reveals an initial perception of erosion. For instance, "The rocks are where the rivers were" and "I saw water carving out the canyon" describe some effects of erosion. Through subsequent investigations in this unit, he and his classmates will construct an understanding of this concept.

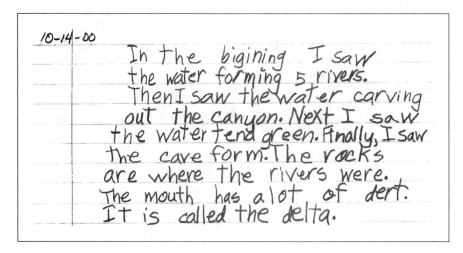

FIGURE 4–4 Jayred's notebook entry

After students have become skilled at making observations and thinking about good questions, they will not need so much guidance. Experiencing inquiry, hearing the kinds of scientific questions a teacher asks, and acting on their natural curiosity, students will end each observation session by discussing some of their own questions, some of which may lead to further investigations depending on time and the situation. (The section about the engagement stage of the teaching-learning sequence in Chapter 2 provides some scaffolding for helping students plan their own investigations.)

Drawing Scientific Illustrations

After students have had plenty of time to observe something carefully, then you can model how to make a scientific illustration. Generally, detailed illustrations work best in life science, and sometimes earth science. (Diagrams tend to be more useful in physical science, as explained in the next section.) For example, students need to observe a plant closely in order to see all its parts and understand their functions. To make detailed scientific illustrations, students must focus as they observe, which helps them increase their observational skills and, subsequently, the quality of both their conceptual understanding and their written observations.

Before students learn how to draw a scientific illustration, they need to understand the difference between an artistic representation of something and a scientific illustration. One approach to teaching this distinction is to ask students to "draw a picture" of a flower at the top of a page, as Brendan, a fourth grader, did in Figure 4–5. Then give them real flowers to observe closely, followed by a minilesson about how to make a scientific illustration, which they will draw below the artistic version. The contrast of the two drawings illustrates the differences between the two ways of representing a flower, both of which are valuable.

Having students draw what they think something looks like before they have closely studied it is also beneficial as an engagement part of a lesson or investigation (for example, drawing a cloud before investigating different types of clouds in a weather unit). When students compare their initial drawing with an illustration they draw after they have closely observed and investigated something, they realize what they have learned.

When you first model how to make a scientific illustration, be sure to involve the students in the process, asking them what they have observed as you model how they might draw what they have seen. This is the same process we use in shared writing: students provide the content of the writing while the teacher models the strategies and the structure. Just as in a writing minilesson, this shared-drawing experience should not be merely a copying exercise. During the lesson, emphasize that students should make their drawings large, accurate, and detailed, and they should label them clearly.

Many students will be less intimidated and more focused in drawing a scientific illustration if you break the process into steps. Start by asking

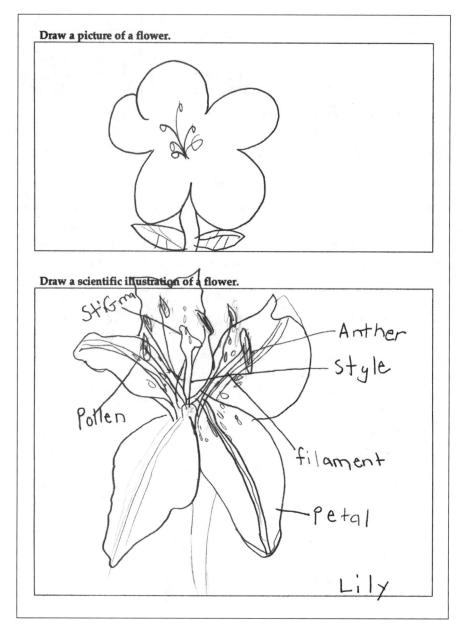

Draw a picture of a flower.

Draw a scientific illustration of a flower.

Stigma

Anther

Style

Pollen

filament

Petal

Lily

FIGURE 4–5 Brendan's drawing and scientific illustration

them about the shape or outside contour of what they are observing. Show them how you would draw what they are describing, noting that their illustration will look different depending on their particular sample. Then divide the object into parts so students can focus on details in each area, in a similar way to what was described with the stream table in Figure 4–3. Also show them how to draw lines that clearly point to or touch the appropriate parts of the illustration, adding labels as necessary. If multiple parts would have the same labels, teach students to label only one of the parts.

In some cases, writing the function of each part next to each label (using a different color to distinguish the function words) can be a useful visual reminder of new science content and terminology, particularly in life science (for example, the parts and their functions in organisms or systems). After you finish with this shared-drawing minilesson, have students make their own scientific illustration in their notebook, following the process you have just modeled. Kindergartners in the fall and winter can draw the illustration in their notebook during the minilesson. Later in the year, they will draw the illustration more independently but still copy the labels.

In the early spring, Kalina, a kindergartner, drew the scientific illustration and caption shown in Figure 4–6. She did not know her letters in the fall nor did any of her classmates. But by the time she makes this entry, she and most of the other kindergartners produce notebook entries like this one on their own. Before drawing and writing, they observe and talk about

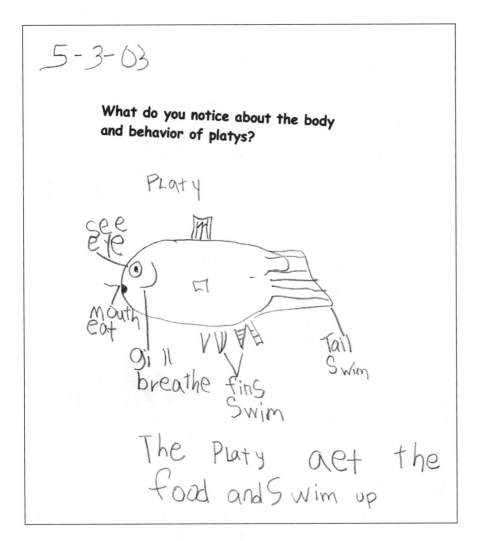

FIGURE 4–6 Kalina's scientific illustration and caption

platys during their science investigation, then they discuss as a whole class what they have discovered. In a shared-drawing and writing minilesson similar to the one above, their teacher draws and labels an illustration on the overhead as they share their observations with her. As she labels each part, she uses another color to write in the function of that part, which helps her students learn the content vocabulary. After that, students write in their own notebooks.

Kalina has drawn an illustration under the focus question she glued in the notebook at the beginning of the science session. She copies the labels from her teacher's illustration. Then she writes a caption about what she observed about the platys' behavior. By this time of year, she can write her own caption independently without any sentence starters or writing frames: "The platy aet [ate] the food and swim up."

In some cases, teaching students how to use quadrants to draw accurate illustrations facilitates the inclusion of details. For example, if students are observing minerals, have them take a small piece (for example, three inches by three inches) of blank white paper and fold it in half vertically, then open it up and fold it in half horizontally. Two creases now will divide the paper into quadrants. Next, have students fold a larger piece of scratch paper in the same way, draw a line over each crease, then place the mineral over the lines so that a part of the mineral lies in each quadrant. Figure 4–7 shows Julienny, a third grader, using this strategy.

On the overhead, model how to draw one set of crossing lines or crosshairs so that they make four quadrants. Place a mineral on top of the lines where they intersect so that some part of the mineral is in each quadrant. Next to this grid, draw another set of intersecting lines. You will draw your model illustration of a mineral on these quadrants. Start by asking students to describe the outside line or contour that they see in one quadrant. Show them how to enlarge the drawing rather than making it more like a tracing. Proceed through each quadrant until you have drawn all the outside edges of the mineral.

Next, focus their attention on the details they notice in one quadrant, modeling how to add details to the illustration, including shading and three-dimensional elements. Also show students how to label certain details (for example, fossils or layers) if appropriate. This attention to detail through drawing helps focus the students' observations and teaches them another way to record and communicate what they observe. Even kindergartners can make three-dimensional drawings when they see the modeling. Students should keep in mind, however, that they do not need to spend time trying to make their scientific illustrations perfect.

Drawing Diagrams

In some cases, particularly in physical science as mentioned earlier, simple diagrams are more appropriate than detailed scientific illustrations and often are a necessary complement to expository text. For instance, when

FIGURE 4–7 Julienny makes a quadrant drawing

intermediate students are studying electric circuits, making simple diagrams of circuits can communicate much more in less space than their writing can, although students still need to explain in writing the concepts underlying what the diagrams represent. In modeling how to make diagrams, note the importance of including only essential elements (for example, a simple rectangular shape and the two terminals to represent a D-cell or battery). Without modeling, students tend to include unimportant details, which makes the drawing process laborious instead of a shorthand form of communication.

Primary students also need to make diagrams in certain units of study. In a physical science unit in which second graders explore how objects sink in different liquids, for example, they can draw the objects in the jars of liquids, adding straight, curved, or zigzag lines to represent how the objects sank to the bottom of the jars. This enables young students to communicate details about what happened in a more efficient way than in writing, although each diagram or sets of diagrams include expository text that describes their thinking (for example, "I think the metal objects sink the fastest. I think this is because they are heavy and solid.").

Figures 4–8 and 4–9 show how a diagram can complement a student's written entry about what he has discovered about balancing a beam with cubes. Jason, who is in second grade, drew the diagrams as he finished each part of the investigation. After a shared-writing minilesson, his teacher instructed students either to use words from the focus question in beginning their notebook entry, or copy a sentence starter ("To balance the beam,"), which they then could complete with their own writing. He also asked the students to write about what they did to balance the beam as well

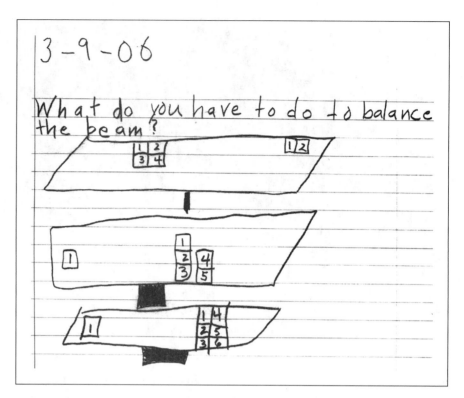

FIGURE 4–8 Jason's diagrams show how he balanced a beam

as what they tried that did not work. Jason's written entry is shown in Figure 4–9.

In the first sentence, Jason describes the middle diagram. He uses *but* to qualify that in putting five cubes on one side and one cube on the other, he had to put the greater number of cubes (the greater mass) closer to the fulcrum and the one cube (lesser mass) farther away from the fulcrum to make the beam balance. The second sentence describes what happened when he did not distribute the mass in that way. Writing about these contrasts helps students think more about what they have discovered, and also gives the teacher a window into their thinking. The diagram helps illustrate what the students are describing in their writing.

Creating and Using Tables

Students also need to learn how to create and use tables for recording data and notes about their observations and investigations. In most cases, students benefit from making their own tables rather than using blackline masters from the teacher or from the teacher's guide. Creating tables helps them internalize some of the science content and also teaches them the valuable scientific skill of organizing observations and other data. Many teachers in the Science Notebooks Program initially are resistant to this idea, either because they believe the students are not developmentally ready for such a task or that the process is not worth the time. But over the

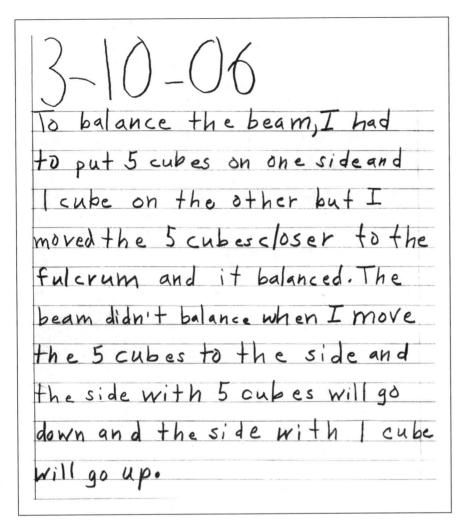

FIGURE 4–9 Jason's written entry

To balance the beam, I had to put 5 cubes on one side and 1 cube on the other but I moved the 5 cubes closer to the fulcrum and it balanced. The beam didn't balance when I move the 5 cubes to the side and the side with 5 cubes will go down and the side with 1 cube will go up.

years, we have found that many teachers discover that their students benefit from creating most tables, and children become increasingly adept at making them as the year progresses.

There are, however, two unproductive ways of teaching students how to make tables. First, students do not need to use a laborious measuring process. Model how to fold pages vertically so that the creases form the columns of a table. If students do this on facing blank pages in a notebook, for instance, they can have two to four columns on each page. Then they can draw the lines down the creases by hand or using a straightedge. Second, do not have them merely copy a table from the overhead or board. Doing so will not teach them anything about the process of making a table. Instead, ask them questions that will lead them through the reasoning process involved in creating a table. By doing so, children will deepen their understanding of the different components of their observations and data collecting.

Figure 4–10 is a kindergarten example of a box chart for collecting data, which Elexis made in her science notebook. Kindergartners in this class make their own simple tables to record data from their controlled investigation, which at this age they call a "fair test." Then they make tally marks to record the results of the tests their group has conducted. In this case, before reporting the results of their investigation about whether earthworms seem to need moist or dry soil, the kindergartners first write about one variable they have to control. The teacher gives them the sentence starter "To make a fair test _____ ." Elexis writes about the need to put the earthworm in the middle—between the moist and dry soil—rather than on one soil or the other, in order to conduct a controlled investigation.

If you know that students will be able to record the information they need in a table that covers only one page, have them make the table on a

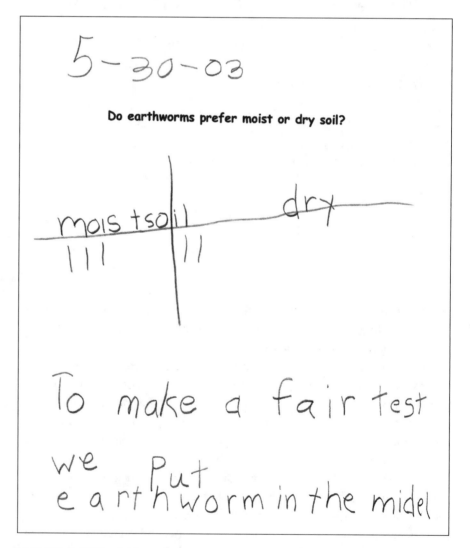

FIGURE 4–10 Elexis' box chart

left-hand page. Then they will be able to look at the table while, on the facing right-hand page, they write about their data or notes.

To make observation and data tables effective tools, students need to learn how to record notes about what they observe rather than write complete sentences or lengthy phrases. After students have set up their tables, model how to make an illustration or diagram, as described earlier, if appropriate. Also model how to write single words or phrases. Learning this notetaking skill will save students of all ages a lot of time and frustration.

Sometimes, students need to record observations of something over a period of time, such as a plant's growth or changes in an aquarium or terrarium. For these ongoing observations, you can create a table on a sheet of unlined, eleven-by-seventeen-inch paper. (In this case, it is appropriate to create this complex table yourself rather than doing it with the students.) Set up the table so that the rows going across the page contain the same type of observation or data. Figure 4–11 shows the illustrations and data that Esa, a third grader, has recorded in her table of ongoing observations of a plant.

As she observes the plant's growth and development every few days, she makes an illustration of the plant and writes notes about her observations and quantitative (measured) data in the adjacent columns. Because the illustrations and data are lined up across the page rather than down the page or on a number of different pages, the changes in the plant over time are much more obvious.

When students write about these observations and data, have them use a separate sheet of paper so they can look at the extended table while they are writing, using it as a prewriting organizer of what to include in their writing. After they are finished, they can glue the sheet onto the next page in their notebook. Again, this approach makes the writing process much easier for the students because they do not have to flip through different pages. This enables them to write more detailed, organized responses.

During investigations in which students need to take notes about their observations, encourage them to spend concentrated time exploring with the materials before they begin drawing and taking notes. The writing should never interfere with their scientific explorations (as explained in the teaching-learning sequence section of Chapter 2).

Writing Observations

By using the Observations organizer to guide their observations, making scientific illustrations or diagrams, and recording data and taking notes in a table, students have conducted and recorded careful observations. The notes they took following the Observations organizer or their table of observations or data now can serve as their prewriting organizers for their written observations.

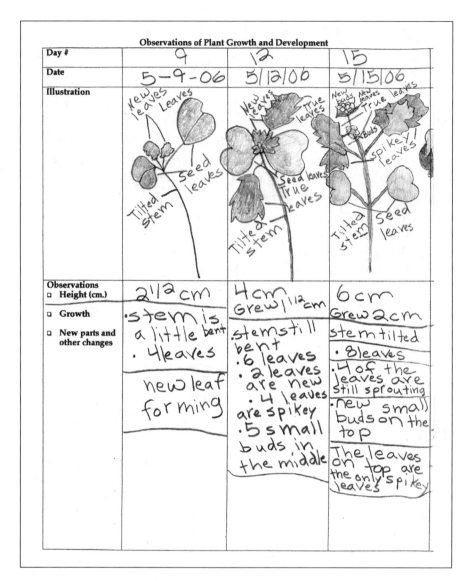

Observations of Plant Growth and Development

Day #	9	12	15
Date	5-9-06	5/12/06	5/15/06
Illustration	*New leaves, Leaves, Seed leaves, Tilted stem*	*New leaves, True leaves, Seed leaves, True leaves, Tilted stem*	*New buds, New leaves, True leaves, Buds, Spikey! leaves, Tilted stem, Seed leaves*
Observations □ Height (cm.) □ Growth □ New parts and other changes	2 1/2 cm • stem is a little bent • 4 leaves new leaf forming	4 cm Grew 1 1/2 cm • stem still bent • 6 leaves • 2 leaves are new • 4 leaves are spikey • 5 small buds in the middle	6 cm Grew 2 cm stem tilted • 8 leaves • 4 of the leaves are still sprouting • new small buds on the top The leaves on top are the only spikey leaves

FIGURE 4–11 Esa's illustrations and notes

In a shared-writing minilesson, you can model how to use these organizers as students write about their scientific observations. Remember that this kind of minilesson almost always occurs in a twenty- to thirty-minute period within a day of the science session (as described in the shared-writing minilesson section of Chapter 2). Begin by reviewing with the students what they discussed during the earlier reflective class discussion. Then, referring to the Observations organizer, for example, ask students what they noticed in terms of each section of the organizer. Write the words "I observed" or "I noticed" to model some useful phrases for this type of writing, then add what the students tell you. If, in a description of an isopod, for instance, a child says, "It's gray. It looks like an oval, too," then you can repeat his observation beginning with the introductory words you have just written: "I observed that the isopod is gray and shaped like an oval." In this way, the students provide the *content* of the writing while you provide some of the *structure and phrasing*. To begin the next sentence, you might write "In addition," then ask students what else they have observed. Continue with "I also noticed" and so on. In this way, students learn transitional phrases to use in their speaking and writing. The "Increasing Sentence Fluency and Independent Writing Skills" section at the end of this chapter includes suggestions for other words and phrases that students can choose in order to increase their fluency and independent writing skills.

When you finish modeling, students write in their notebooks either in a guided way or more independently. Remove the shared-writing example. Then, to help those who need some structure, write a frame from your modeling on the overhead or board. From this example you would write: "I observed _____ . In addition, _____ . I also noticed _____ ." Have students refer to their own notes, and the Observations organizer if necessary, as they complete the frame with their own observations. Remind them that they can use their own words as well as words from the classroom environment (for example, the science word bank, and class charts and tables). Also make it clear that the length of the lines does not represent the length of their sentences nor does the writing necessarily end with just the three sentences. The frame is there only to help them get started. And they do not need to use it at all if they can write well without it.

Written Observations from Primary Students

Looking at student notebook entries from a variety of units and from students who are in various stages of development in language and in writing can illustrate more about how we can help students learn to write about their observations. Samsam, an ELL student who is just beginning first grade, wrote the observation in Figure 4–12. Her teacher has modeled how to observe one seed and take notes about it in a table that includes four columns, each with an icon that represents one of four senses: sight, touch, smell, and hearing. (The class is studying *Organisms*, a unit published by STC.) After the modeling, students observe the different seeds, then take simple notes in the table, which they have glued into their notebook. Then they have a reflective class discussion during which students refer to their notes as they talk about the seeds. (Students do not learn the names of the seeds until later in the unit.)

In a separate shared-writing minilesson, the teacher models how to write about the students' observations of one seed using the table in the notebook as a prewriting organizer. She also models how to use the science word bank and inventive spelling to write the sentences. Then students write their own observation in their notebook.

Note how using the table helps Samsam write quite a detailed description of her seed: "I see white owal [oval] long big seeb [seed] The seeb feels smooth and it do not smell it do not have tap nsi [tapping noises]". She first includes several details about what she has observed with her sight: color,

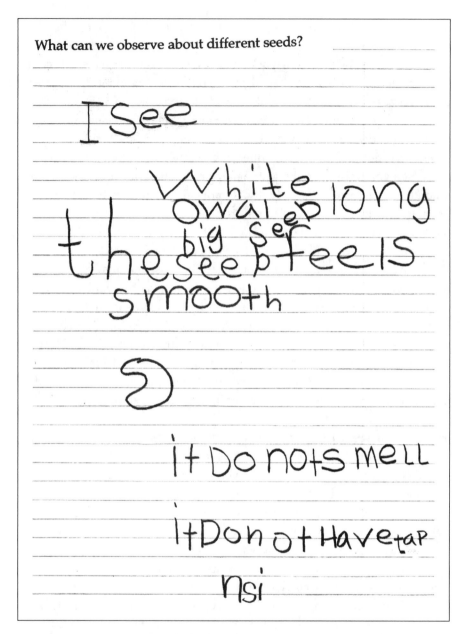

What can we observe about different seeds?

I See

white oblong
owal
big seeb
the seeb feels
smooth

It Do not smell

It Don ot Have tap
nsi

FIGURE 4–12 Samsam's seed observation

shape, and size. These characteristics are listed in the Observations organizer. The last three sections of her entry include details—texture, odor, and
sounds—discovered through using three other senses. She draws a simple
illustration as well. On the whole, this is a detailed, organized, thoughtful
entry from a young student who is learning English. She will learn more
about conventions of capitalization, punctuation, and sentence structure as
her writing develops.

Figure 4–13 illustrates the importance of teaching students to describe
what they have observed as a way to explain how they have determined
something. After an investigation and class discussion in *Balls and Ramps*,

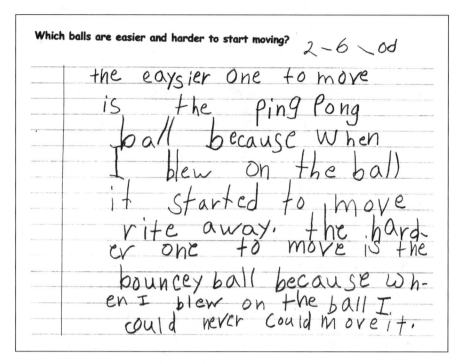

Which balls are easier and harder to start moving? 2-6 od

the eaysier one to move
is the ping pong
ball because When
I blew on the ball)
it started to move
rite away. the hard-
er one to move is the
bouncey ball because wh-
en I blew on the ball I
could never could move it.

FIGURE 4–13 Kimberly's notebook entry

a unit published by Insights, the teacher in this class of first graders gave her students two sentence starters: "The easier one to move is _____ because _____ . The harder one to move is _____ because _____ ."

First graders with strong writing skills generally do not need sentence starters. Instead, they can learn to use words from the focus question to begin their responses, adding *because* as a reminder to describe what happened with each ball. In this notebook entry, Kimberly identifies which ball is easier or harder to move. Using the word *because* prompts her to include what happened when she blew on the ball, a cause-effect relationship that she includes to substantiate her claim that one ball was easier and the other ball was harder to move.

To write about other observations of cause and effect, students who are beginning to learn how to write—young students as well as ELL and special education students—can write successfully by beginning sentences with introductory clauses such as "When I" and "After I," which organize their thinking and writing. In Figure 4–14, Adrianna, a second grader who struggles with writing, reports what she has observed as she investigates how a drop of syrup behaves in a jar of water (a lesson in *Liquids*, a unit published by Insights). After a shared-writing minilesson, the teacher writes the following frame on the overhead for those students who need it: "First, when I added _____ , I observed _____ . After stirring, I noticed _____ . After the liquid rested, _____ ."

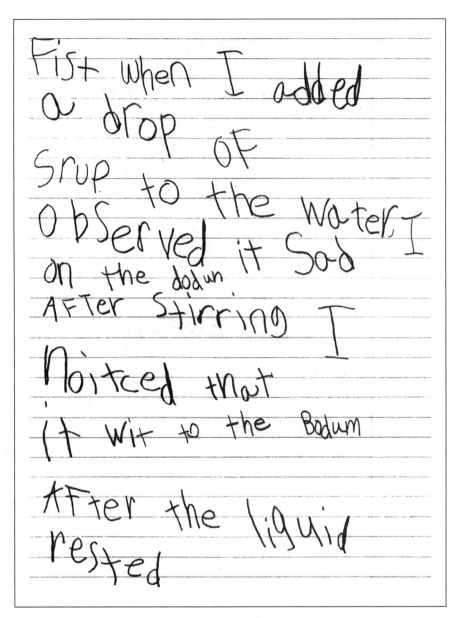

FIGURE 4–14 Adrianna's observations of cause and effect

Adrianna then uses the frame to structure her response: "Fist [First] when I added a drop of srup [syrup] to the water, I observed it sad [sat] on the dodun [bottom]. After stirring I noitced that it wit [went] to the Bodum [bottom]. After the liquid rested." She does not finish the entry, which is a realistic result sometimes when students who struggle with writing are trying to complete a notebook entry during a certain time frame. But what is important to discuss with her is not the weakness of her entry but its strengths: She uses the frame effectively so her observation is organized, and she reports her observations about two parts of the investigation. Her teacher can point out these strengths, then ask Adrianna, "What happened to the drop of syrup after it rested?" and "What would you want to tell another scientist about your observations?" Adrianna then can add to her entry.

Figure 4–15 is another sample about a different liquid in this investigation. Duncan, a strong student in the same second-grade class, is able to write more details about his observations during the independent writing session. He also includes a conclusion about the investigation: "Oil and water dont mix." Now that Duncan has had some experience writing in this way with the frame, he should be able to write independently just by using the cause-and-effect structure of his investigation: When I did this to a liquid, then this happened.

A Fifth Grader's Written Observations

Michelle, a fifth grader with strong writing skills, wrote the entry shown in Figure 4–16. Her teacher had asked the students to write about their observations of isopods and crickets, which they were investigating during the *Ecosystems* unit, published by STC. Students in this class write their observations independently, but initially they use the Observations organizer in making and recording their observations, which is evident in the kinds of details that Michelle includes in the first few sentences as she describes the

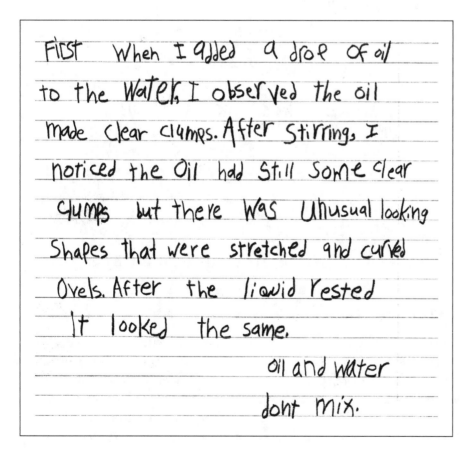

FIGURE 4–15 Duncan's liquids observations

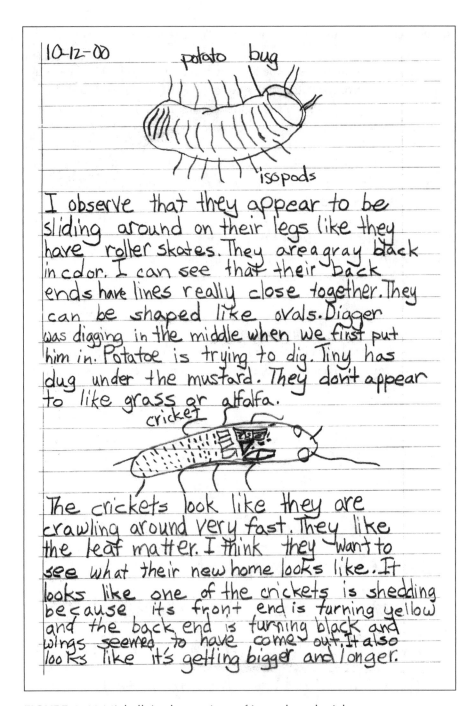

FIGURE 4–16 Michelle's observations of isopods and crickets

movement, color, lines, and shape of the isopods' bodies. She then does what most elementary students do when they talk and write about animals: She humanizes them, giving them names and imaginary lives. This is understandable but problematic, especially when students make inferences without backing them up with evidence. The descriptions of where Digger, Potatoe, and Tiny are digging are appropriate, although using the names is questionable.

The last sentence in the first paragraph exemplifies another common issue with student observations: They state inferences without substantiating them with observations or quantitative (measured) data. We would want to ask Michelle, in this case, what she has *observed* that makes her infer that the isopods do not "appear to like grass or alfalfa." Adding the word *because* to her inferential statement would prompt her to add evidence, which in this case is what she actually has observed. To improve the statement, she might add, "because I observed," then write something about her observations, such as "they never went over to the grass or alfalfa." Similarly, in the second sentence of the paragraph about crickets, she writes, "They like leaf matter." Again, if she adds details from her observations or her thinking, she will support her inference, which would be stronger scientific thinking and writing.

The statement also is weak because it is unequivocal: "They like leaf matter." But what is her evidence? By beginning the sentence with "I think," then finishing with words to express her inferential thinking, Michelle will have a structure for writing evidence-supported inferences, which reflect both higher-level thinking and writing. Combining these elements into sentences, she might write, "I think the crickets like leaf matter because I have observed that they keep going back to the leaf matter and now it has holes in it." Notice how she actually does something similar in the fourth sentence about crickets: "It looks like one of the crickets is shedding because its front end is turning yellow and the back end is turning black . . . " She now is supporting her inference with evidence, which is strong scientific thinking and writing.

The final part of the sentence—"it also looks like it's getting bigger and longer"—naturally leads to more scientific investigation if the teacher asks, "What would help you prove to another scientist that the cricket actually is getting bigger and longer?" This question will help Michelle recognize the importance of including quantitative (measured) data in scientific observations without making her feel like she has done something wrong in her writing. After considering these editorial questions and further developing her scientific thinking, she could edit her entry in her notebook. She clearly has made detailed observations and already has strong writing skills; she just needs to learn more about the scientific thinking that will lead to consistently strong *scientific* writing.

Comparisons

Often, to enhance their learning, students need to compare and contrast what they have been observing—objects, organisms, or events, for example. To be able to do this effectively, students first must make detailed, organized observations as described in the previous section. If you know they will be comparing and contrasting the properties or characteristics of two objects, organisms, or events that they have been observing, have students set aside the next two *facing pages* in the science notebook. On the left-hand page, they can make an illustration or diagram and write an observation, and on the facing right-hand page, they can draw the other illustration or diagram and write an observation. By setting up the notebook entry in this way, students will be able to see the information on both pages at the same time, which will facilitate the comparison strategy described below.

Box and T-Chart Strategy for Comparisons: Shared-Writing Minilesson

To teach students how to make and write a comparison, you can model this simple strategy using familiar objects, such as an apple and an orange. The benefit of using something familiar is that students can practice the strategy before they begin investigating and learning about something that is unfamiliar. After students have had this initial experience with the strategy, you can use the approach in class discussions about what the students are investigating.

Begin by drawing a box on the board, then write "Same" or "Similar" above it (see Figure 4–17). Ask students how the apple and orange are the

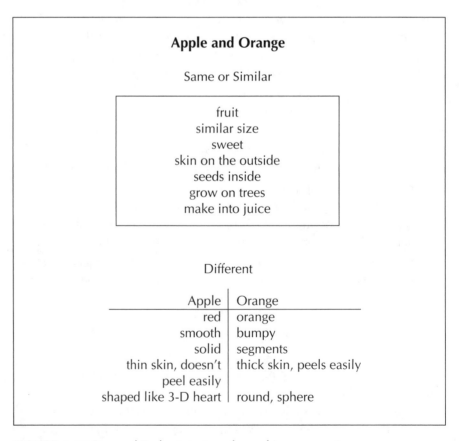

FIGURE 4–17 Box and T-chart strategy for making comparisons

same or similar, writing each characteristic in the box as the students say it. Have students refer to the Observations organizer if they need more ideas. Also, if students do not mention it, ask them in what larger category the objects belong (fruit in this case) and put that at the top of the list in the box. Learning about classification is an integral part of developing scientific thinking.

Below the box, make a T-chart, with "Apple" at the top of one column and "Orange" at the top of the other column. As students mention a difference, be sure they understand that you are adding each characteristic to the chart by category rather than randomly. Often, students will say only one characteristic, such as "The apple is red." Ask about the contrasting characteristic: "So the color of the apple is red. What color is the orange?" As you add the contrasting characteristic, repeat both as sentences, using contrasting words between the two columns (for example, "The apple is red, *but* the orange is orange. The apple is smooth, *whereas* the orange is bumpy.") In this way, you orally model the language that students will need to learn for writing comparisons. Students also typically will say something vague, such as "It is red." Be sure to ask them to identify the antecedent for *it*. If we make them aware of this problem during discussions, students will be less likely to make the mistake in their writing.

The completed box and T-chart now can become a prewriting organizer for a comparison. To model how to write a comparison, put the Compare and Contrast writing frame (see Figure 4–18) on the board next to the completed box and T-chart. On the overhead, model how to use the box and the writing frame (noted in italicized words) to begin the comparison. Write the first part of the frame: "*The* apple *and the* orange *are similar because they both* . . . ." Now ask the class how they could complete the sentence using words that they contributed to the box (for example, "are fruit that taste sweet."). Then tell them, as you write "In addition," that this phrase helps us add information to our writing. Ask them what they could write next about the similarities between an apple and an orange. The completed paragraph might look something like this: "*In addition, they* are a similar size and they have skin on the outside and seeds inside. Also, they both grow on trees and can be made into juice."

Next, model how to write the contrasts, using the T-chart and the words you used during the first part of the minilesson along with student suggestions. The contrasts might look like this:

They are different because the apple is red, *but the* orange is orange. *Also,* the apple is smooth, *whereas* the orange is bumpy. Furthermore, the apple is solid, but the orange has segments. The apple has thin skin that does not peel easily, whereas the orange has thick skin that peels off quite easily. The apple is the shape of a three-dimensional heart. The orange is shaped like a sphere.

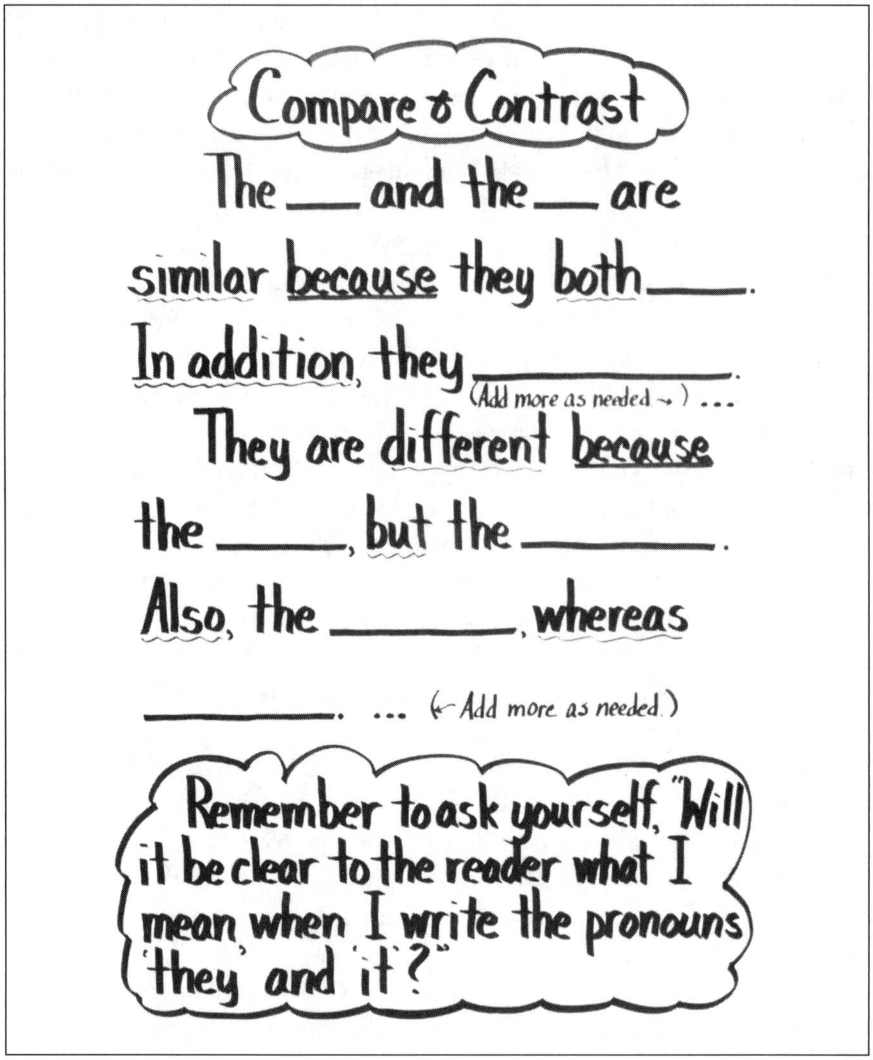

FIGURE 4–18 Wall chart of Compare and Contrast writing frame

After this minilesson, students can work in pairs to make their own box and T-charts to compare and contrast objects, organisms, or events that they have been observing and investigating. Because they need to see both illustrations or diagrams and written observations on facing pages in their notebook as they are filling in their box and T-chart, have them use a separate sheet of lined paper to make the organizer. After they have completed it, they can glue it onto the next left-hand page in their notebook, then write their comparison on the facing right-hand page. When students easily can see the information in one place, they can create more complete organizers and then include more details in an organized way in their written comparisons. Many students will be able to look up at the wall to use the writing frame. Others will be more successful if they use their own copy of a blackline master of this frame, which is included in Appendix A.

The Compare and Contrast frame is effective as an initial scaffolding, particularly for ELL and special education students, although it also helps students with more developed skills write more organized, detailed comparisons than they typically write on their own. However, the frame also results in robotic writing. At some point, depending on your students' language skills, have other minilessons to show students how to write more fluently and independently. For example, after an editing minilesson in which students learn how to combine simple sentences that include similar characteristics and after they have learned more transitional phrases, the shared writing might look like this:

> The apple and the orange have many similarities and differences. They are similar because they both are sweet-tasting fruit that grow on trees and are made into juice. In addition, they are the same size, and have skin on the outside and seeds on the inside.
>
> The apple and orange also are different in many ways. The apple is red, smooth, and shaped like a three-dimensional heart. In contrast, the orange is orange, bumpy, and shaped like a sphere. Furthermore, the apple's skin does not peel off easily and the inside is solid, whereas the orange's skin peels off quite easily and the inside is made up of segments that come apart readily.

The "Increasing Sentence Fluency and Independent Writing Skills" section at the end of this chapter addresses other ways to help students write more fluently and independently.

Examples of Written Comparisons by Primary Students

Figure 4–19 is an example of a comparison written by a kindergartner named Chardonay. Throughout the year, her teacher, whose students begin the year not knowing their letters, has continually modeled using inventive spelling and words in the environment (for example, the science word bank, high-frequency words in the word wall, and class charts) as they write together. By winter, the teacher can provide a simple frame after a shared-writing minilesson, and most of her students are able to copy the frame and write the rest independently. They also are thoroughly familiar with the box and T-chart strategy because the teacher has used it frequently in class discussions and modeled how to make comparisons both orally and in writing. Consequently, by spring, most of her students no longer need a frame.

In this sample, which Chardonay writes in March, the class has just been observing, then comparing and contrasting, two types of worms in the *Animals Two by Two* unit, published by FOSS. The teacher gives the students the following frame: "Both worms have _____ . The _____ , but the _____ ." Despite using the frame, the student writing is varied. Note how Chardonay contrasts two characteristics in the same category—the color of the underside of the body. Students who learn to create a

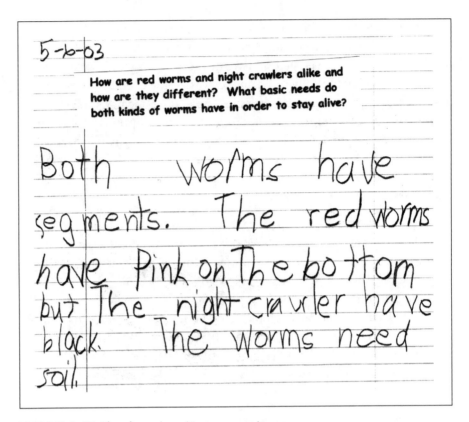

5-16-03

How are red worms and night crawlers alike and how are they different? What basic needs do both kinds of worms have in order to stay alive?

Both worms have segments. The red worms have pink on the bottom but the night crawler have black. The worms need soil.

FIGURE 4–19 Chardonay's written comparison

T-chart, then use it in writing about contrasts, become adept at making contrasts like this. Without the organizer, students tend to compare different characteristics or properties (for example, the color of the red worm with the length of the night crawler). Chardonay finishes her entry by choosing to write about something that both worms need—soil.

The notebook entry in Figure 4–20 is written by Anh, a first grader who in February transitioned to the classroom from the school district's Bilingual Orientation Center for non-English-speaking students who are new to the district. Anh knew only about 10 sight words when she arrived in class, but by June learned all 120 words in the district's list. In this class, her teacher values science as a content area as well as a means of teaching students how to write expository text, so students are immersed in science investigations throughout the week. They do much of their daily writing in science.

After a class discussion about an investigation the students had done in *Organisms*, a unit published by STC, the teacher models a shared-writing minilesson. Students then write their comparisons of plants and animals using the Compare and Contrast frame, which always is posted on the wall. Anh has had so much experience with comparisons now that she can choose what she wants from the class box and T-chart and use as much of the frame as she needs to as she writes. Except for not including how the

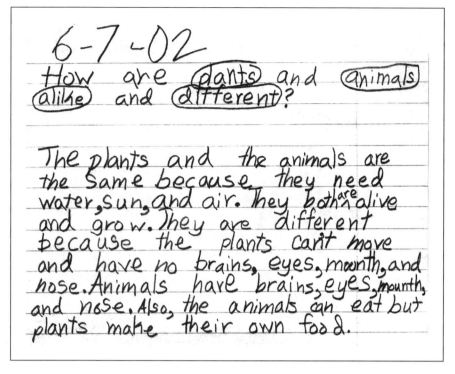

6-7-02
How are (plants) and (animals)
(alike) and (different)?

The plants and the animals are
the same because they need
water, sun, and air. They both are alive
and grow. They are different
because the plants can't move
and have no brains, eyes, moonth, and
nose. Animals have brains, eyes, mounth,
and nose. Also, the animals can eat but
plants make their own food.

FIGURE 4–20 Anh's notebook entry

animals move as a contrast to the statement "the plants can't move," she
has written a strong comparison.

Figure 4–21 shows how a special education student benefits from using
the structure of the box and T-chart and a writing frame in October of second
grade. In this class, the students have been investigating the similarities and
differences between liquids and solids. (The teacher is using *Liquids*, a unit
published by Insights. District science specialists and scientists have developed some lessons about solids to add to the unit in order to meet some
specific state science standards.) After a shared reflection about the investigations with solids, the class creates a box and T-chart together. Students
talk in pairs first, then share their ideas with the class. The teacher writes
the similarities and differences in the organizer as students share them.
Afterward, the children write independently using the Compare and Contrast frame posted in the room.

Derrick, the student who writes this entry and generally struggles with
writing, includes two important similarities between liquids and solids:
"thy [they] can pour" and they "take the shape of the container." Then,
departing from the frame and still recording a difference, he writes, "liquids flow freely froom one container to another and the particles pours in
clump." In the second month of second grade, Derrick is writing quite successfully about his understanding of a concept. The box and T-chart and
writing frame serve as scaffolding that help him develop some confidence

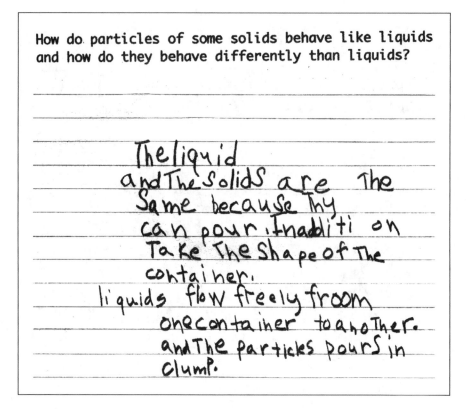

How do particles of some solids behave like liquids and how do they behave differently than liquids?

The liquid and The solids are The Same because Thy can pour.Inaddition Take The Shape of The container.
liquids flow freely froom one container to another. and The particks pours in clump.

FIGURE 4–21 Derrick's compare-contrast entry

in his writing abilities, which will be the most essential part of his early growth as a writer. With students who struggle with writing, the teacher focuses on the strengths in the writing. After Derrick develops additional skills, his teacher can ask questions that will help him improve in his weaker areas.

Sharmaine, a student in this class who has developed strong language skills, uses the same frame in writing the entry shown in Figure 4–22. We cannot tell just from the writing whether Sharmaine has more conceptual understanding at this point than Derrick or if she just is able to write a longer entry. But it is apparent that the box and T-chart organizer and wording from the frame help her organize her writing and articulate her ideas. With a student who has such strong skills, the teacher would want to help her learn how to combine sentences and use additional transition words. In class minilessons about writing comparisons, for example, her teacher could write an entry like this and ask the class, "What are some *other ways* we could write this comparison?" We do not want students to become dependent on the frames, thus limiting their sentence fluency and independence.

Figure 4–23 shows that Dezmarie, a third grader, has learned how to use a box and T-chart to organize a comparison of two minerals (in *Rocks and Minerals*, a unit published by STC). Notice in the T-chart how she checks off

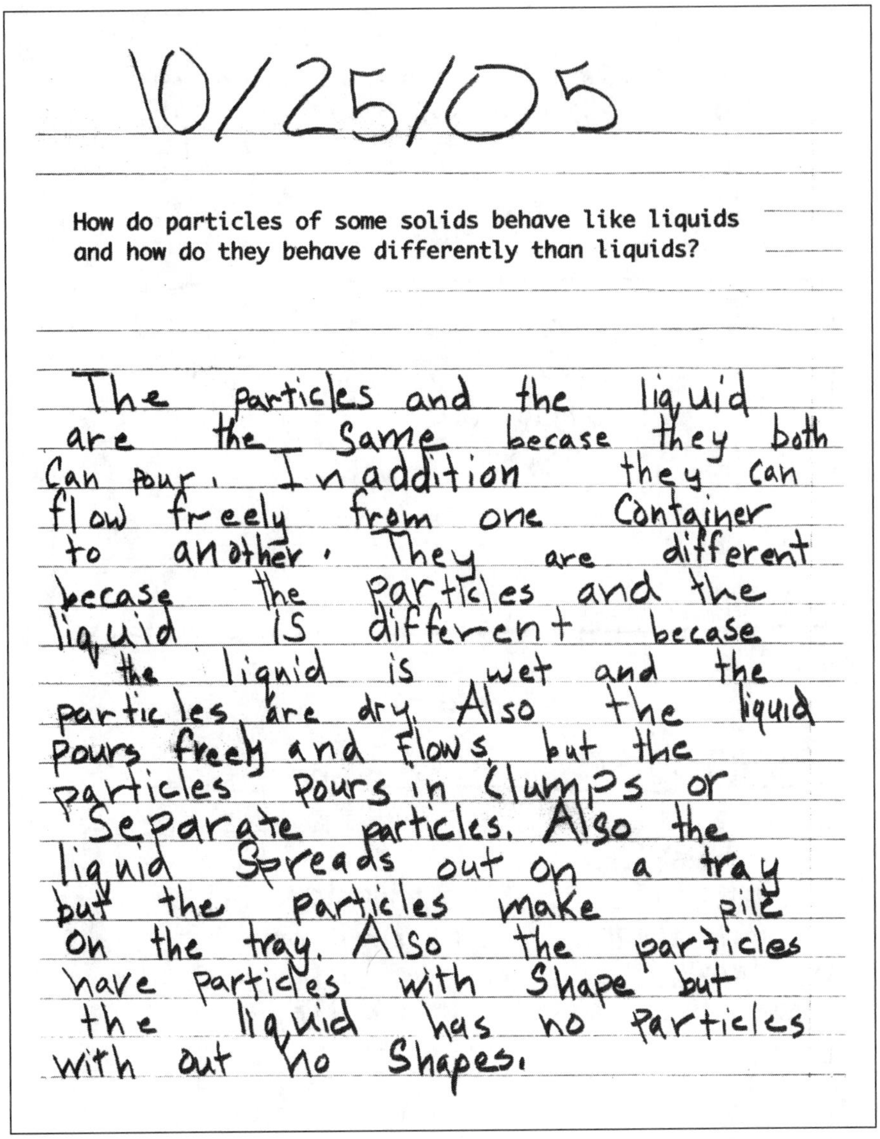

10/25/05

How do particles of some solids behave like liquids and how do they behave differently than liquids?

The particles and the liquid are the same becase they both can pour. In addition they can flow freely from one container to another. They are different becase the particles and the liquid is different becase the liquid is wet and the particles are dry. Also the liquid pours freely and flows but the particles pours in clumps or separate particles. Also the liquid spreads out on a tray but the particles make pile on the tray. Also the particles have particles with shape but the liquid has no particles with out no shapes.

FIGURE 4–22 Sharmaine's entry

the properties as she addresses them in her writing. Her teacher has taught the students to use this strategy so they will include more details.

Figure 4–24 shows Dezmarie's written comparison, which she writes independently, having moved beyond the writing frame. She has learned to contrast properties from the same categories (shape, hardness, color, and texture). Even though notebook entries are rough drafts, this entry is a thorough, organized comparison based on the observations the student has made of the two minerals.

Comparisons: Writing About Change Over Time

The T-chart organizer, which really is just a simple table, also supports students when they need to write about how something has changed over time

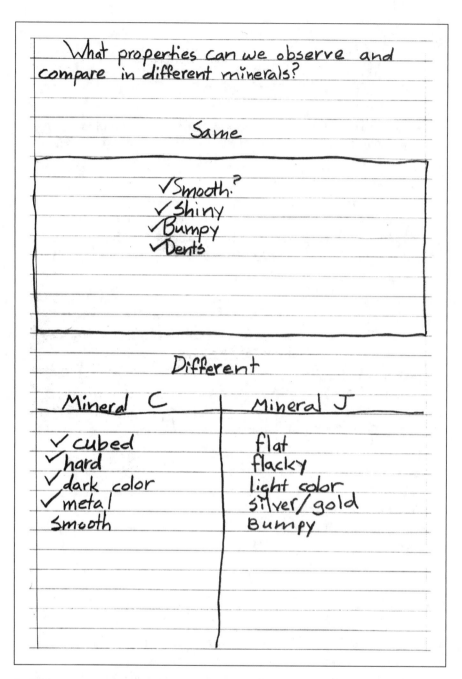

FIGURE 4–23 Dezmarie's box and T-chart

(for example, the growth and development of a plant during its life cycle, or changes in a compost bin). It also can illustrate cause and effect such as the effects a particular pollutant has on an ecosystem, as in STC's *Ecosystems* unit, for example. By using a T-chart to record observations about corresponding components of the control ecocolumn (an aquarium and terrarium that are attached) and a polluted ecocolumn, students can clearly see and remember the differences between the two. Then when they write about the contrast,

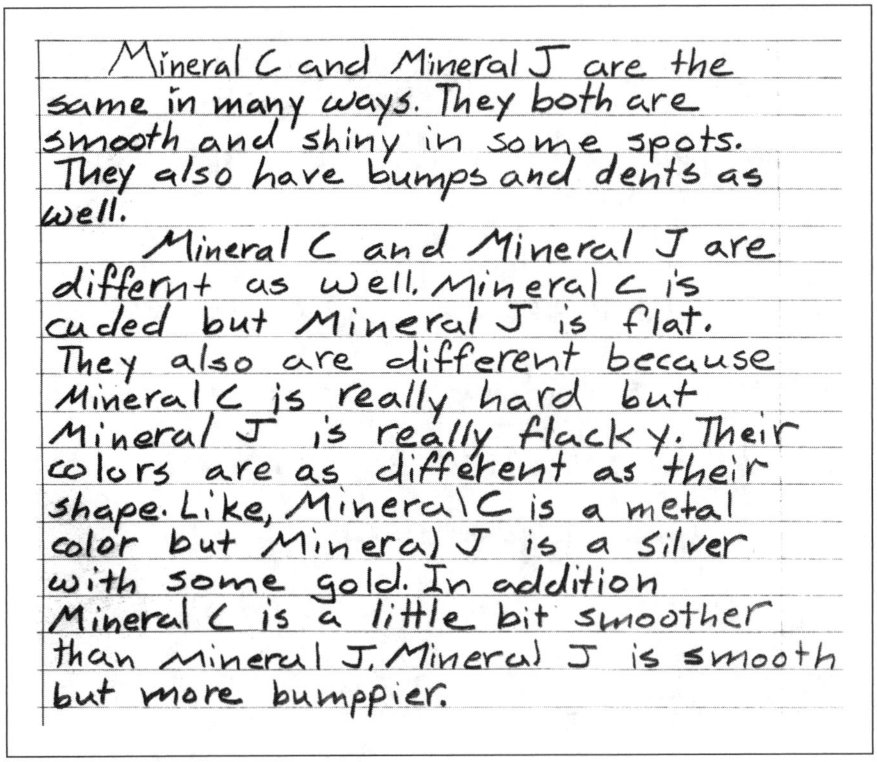

> Mineral C and Mineral J are the same in many ways. They both are smooth and shiny in some spots. They also have bumps and dents as well.
>
> Mineral C and Mineral J are differnt as well. Mineral C is cuded but Mineral J is flat. They also are different because Mineral C is really hard but Mineral J is really flacky. Their colors are as different as their shape. Like, Mineral C is a metal color but Mineral J is a silver with some gold. In addition Mineral C is a little bit smoother than mineral J, Mineral J is smooth but more bumppier.

FIGURE 4–24 Dezmarie's written comparison

which also is the evidence of the effects of a pollutant, they can write an organized report with a conclusion. (These more complex comparisons, which actually are conclusions, are explained in the next chapter.)

The entry in Figure 4–25 is from the notebook of Edgar, a bilingual third grader who is reporting the changes he has observed in his plant between day 27 and day 33 of his investigation. (Day 1 was the day he planted the seed.) He has been recording his ongoing observations on an eleven-by-seventeen-inch table, as described in the "Creating and Using Tables" section of this chapter and shown in Figure 4–11. (These investigations are part of the *Plant Growth and Development* unit, published by STC.) Edgar has recorded his notes in his table in an organized way so that his observations about the seed pods, for example, are written on the same line in adjacent columns. For each part, he can contrast what he observed on day 27 with what he notices on day 33. Consequently, he is using the two columns of his table as a T-chart as he compares and, thus, notes the changes over time in the seed pods, flowers, leaves, and stem.

Note that Edgar has learned the transition words *first, then, next,* and *finally* to structure his observation. His teacher has been modeling these words in class discussions and shared-writing minilessons, so her students are familiar with their use. He also has learned to use contrasting words such as *but* and *on the other hand* in between each set of contrasts.

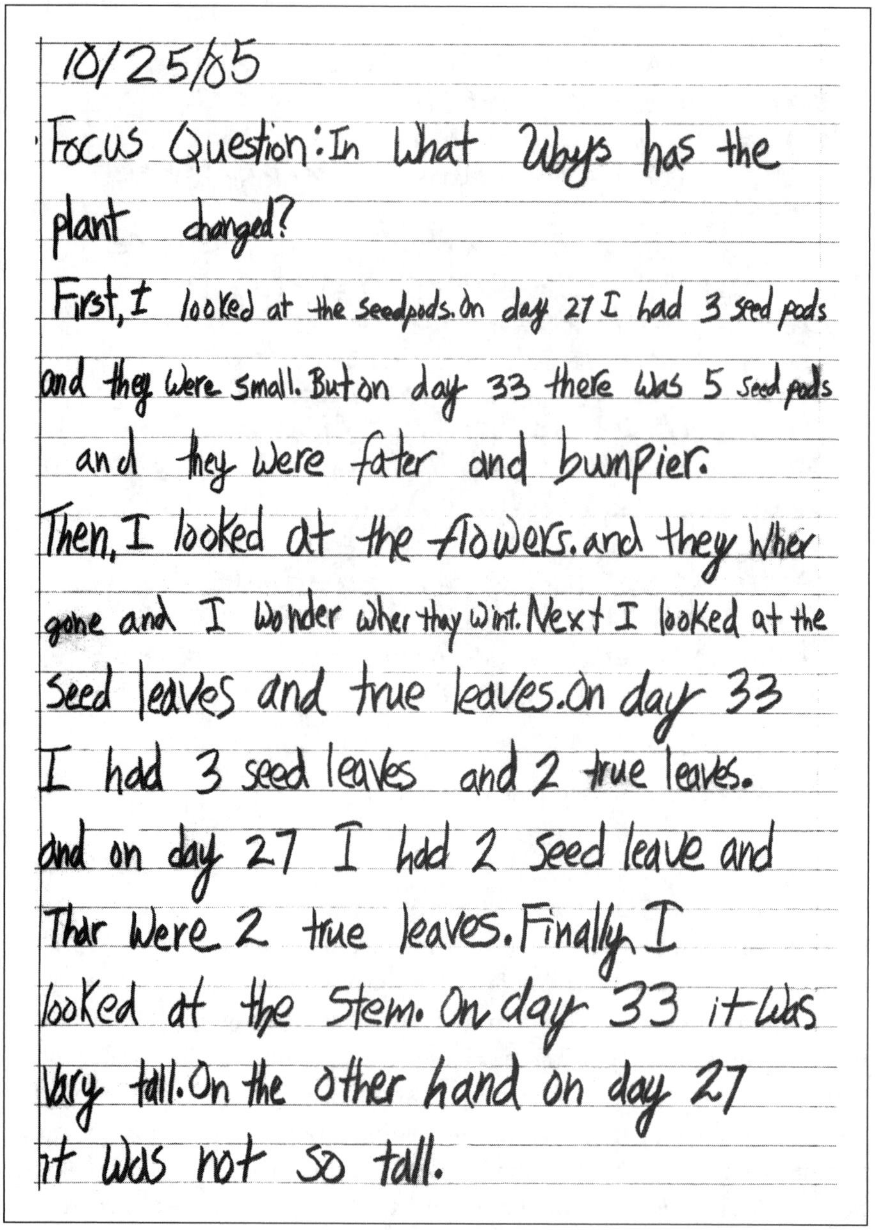

> 10/25/05
>
> Focus Question: In what ways has the plant changed?
>
> First, I looked at the seedpods. On day 27 I had 3 seed pods and they were small. But on day 33 there was 5 seed pods and they were fater and bumpier.
>
> Then, I looked at the flowers. and they wher gone and I wonder wher thay wint. Next I looked at the seed leaves and true leaves. On day 33 I had 3 seed leaves and 2 true leaves. and on day 27 I had 2 seed leave and ther were 2 true leaves. Finally I looked at the stem. On day 33 it was vary tall. On the other hand on day 27 it was not so tall.

FIGURE 4–25 Edgar's observations of plant growth and development

At this point, Edgar is focusing on observing and noting the changes in the plant. By the end of the unit, he will develop an understanding of how these changes actually constitute the plant's life cycle and are not, as he may have previously thought, random.

Increasing Sentence Fluency and Independent Writing Skills

As students learn to write scientifically using writing frames and other scaffolding, they can become dependent on such structures even when they have the skills to write independently. A variety of strategies can help them develop more independence and greater sentence fluency.

One simple strategy is to teach them to read the question to which they are responding, if there is one, then use the words from the question in their topic sentence. (They should be aware, however, that this strategy does not work with every question.) Focusing on the question also will help them understand it and respond appropriately.

Another strategy, as has been mentioned earlier, is to model effective language in class discussions so that students can develop "an ear" for what the words and phrases sound like. Particularly in classes with ELL students, ask children to repeat the new words with you while you hold up a word card, so everyone can see the word or phrase as you are speaking. Students will be more successful in independently using new language in their writing if they have heard and spoken it a number of times beforehand.

A useful approach for developing students' independent writing skills is to create a class chart that includes a variety of words and phrases they can use in their writing, as shown in Figure 4–26. You can develop the chart over time with the class, adding new sections, words, and phrases as students have a need to know them. Also, as you and the students read informational text, have them look for new words and phrases to add to the chart.

Modeling thinking aloud during the shared-writing minilesson is also an important practice for developing students' independence in writing. For example, you might say, "You have shared more details in your observations. What are some words or phrases we can use to add information to the description we have written so far?" Students could look at the Adding Information section of the class chart and offer such transition words and phrases as *Also*, *In addition*, and *Furthermore*.

Over time, students will look at the chart only to double-check their spelling. Finally, they will use the words all on their own, using the chart only when they discover words and phrases they want to add to it.

Useful Words and Phrases in Scientific Writing

Questions	Observations	Contrasts	Sequence of Time, Cause and Effect, Reasoning
What would happen if _____?	I observed	_____, but _____.	First, _____.
How does [the changed variable] affect [the measured, observed, responding variable]?	I noticed	_____, whereas _____.	Next, _____.
	When _____, _____.	However,	Then, _____.
	After _____, _____.	In contrast,	Finally, _____.
		At first, _____.	If _____, then _____.
		But now, _____.	So, _____.
			This leads to
			As a result,
			Consequently,

Evidence	Reasoning	Adding Information, Evidence, Reasoning	Conclusions
_____ because _____.	_____ because _____.	Also,	Therefore, I think
For example,	I think this because	In addition,	In conclusion, I think
For instance,	I think this means	Furthermore,	Therefore,
The evidence is			In conclusion,
The data show			
The data provide evidence that			

Note to teachers: Students can become too dependent on sentence starters and writing frames that teachers provide. To support students in becoming more independent writers, you can post a chart like this in the classroom, adding words and phrases as needed. Also teach students to use words from questions as appropriate in beginning their responses.

FIGURE 4–26 Chart for increasing fluency and independent writing

CHAPTER FIVE

Teaching Complex Forms of Scientific Thinking and Expository Writing

Reasoning, Data Analysis, and Conclusions

To write proficiently about their reasoning, and to explain their thinking about data and their conclusions, students first must have ample time to work with concrete materials, conduct and talk about their investigations, and hear and use appropriate scientific thinking and language as they construct their understanding. Then, during a shared-writing minilesson, they revisit their thinking and learn the writing structures and frames that can scaffold their written entries. Such scaffolding can help students remember what they need to include in this more complex writing, and provide effective words and phrases for these new types of scientific expression.

This chapter explains what we have learned in the Science Notebooks Program about teaching students to write scientifically about their reasoning and conclusions. The process begins with the teaching and learning of the word *because* as a prompt for providing reasoning. This leads to identifying the components of data analysis and scientific conclusions and how these components increase in complexity as students progress from kindergarten through fifth grade.

Providing Evidence with *Because*

In learning to write effectively about their scientific thinking, young students need to understand the necessity of providing evidence for their statements. One of the simplest but most powerful skills students can learn in science discussions and writing is to use the word *because*, then express reasoning for their thinking. Hundreds of teachers who have participated in the Science Notebooks Program have said that teaching their students—

from kindergarten through fifth grade—to use *because* as a way to prompt them to express their reasoning has dramatically affected the quality of the students' oral and written communication. This also helps teachers assess their students' conceptual understanding because students actually remember to include their thoughts.

Using *because* in predictions is an example of how the word can help students provide reasoning for their thoughts, which may also cause students to think more deeply about what they are predicting and writing. Kimberly wrote the prediction shown in Figure 5–1. In early fall of first grade, she is to predict what she thinks an isopod will do when placed between a sample of dry soil and another of moist soil. Typically, a young student simply would write the first part: "I predict the isopod will go on the moist soil." But by adding the word *because*, Kimberly has to tell the reader why she is making that prediction: "becaus moist is water and nuthing can servive with out water." The words that follow *because* provide her teacher with some insight into Kimberly's prior knowledge and her ability to use it in her reasoning, which is sophisticated for a student who is just beginning first grade.

To elicit this type of entry from her students, Kimberly's teacher first has a planning session in which the students discuss how they will set up a "fair test" (controlled investigation) for their investigative question, "Do isopods need moist or dry soil in their habitat?" (This is a controlled investigation that the science program has added to *Organisms*, a unit published by Science and Technology for Children or STC.) After students discuss all the things they have to "keep the same" (controlled variables) and how all

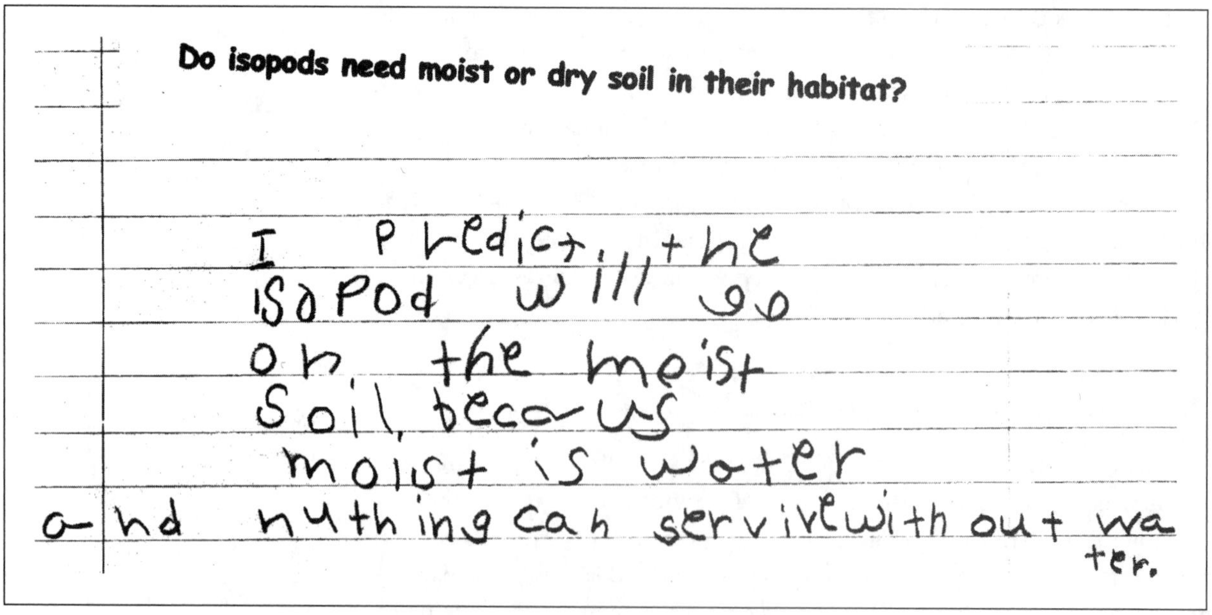

Do isopods need moist or dry soil in their habitat?

I predict the isopod will go on the moist soil, becaus moist is water and nuthing can servive with out water.

FIGURE 5–1 Kimberly's prediction and reasoning

the groups will conduct the investigation, they set up their T-charts for recording how many times their isopod goes to the moist and the dry soil. Before students begin conducting the tests, the teacher provides a simple prediction frame for them to use as they write a prediction in their science notebook: "I predict _____ because _____ ."

Later in the unit, students observe "mystery animals," which they eventually will learn are the larvae of mealworm beetles, and make predictions about what changes they think they will observe. By this time, many students routinely provide reasoning for their predictions without any prompt. In Figure 5–2, Kimberly's second prediction reveals a precocious vocabulary and background knowledge. She predicts the mystery animal "will grow becaus food mateerisise [materializes] in to a nootrishin [nutrition] and makes you grow." Again, the word *because* prompts her to explain her prediction, which allows her teacher to understand how Kimberly is thinking. In this case, the teacher realizes that Kimberly has highly developed language skills and rich background knowledge.

With students like this, a teacher's challenge is to convince them that they need to provide reasoning—including evidence—for their thinking. While this inferential thinking is not a significant problem in making predictions, it does become an issue when students are writing more complex entries in which they need to present evidence from their investigations to

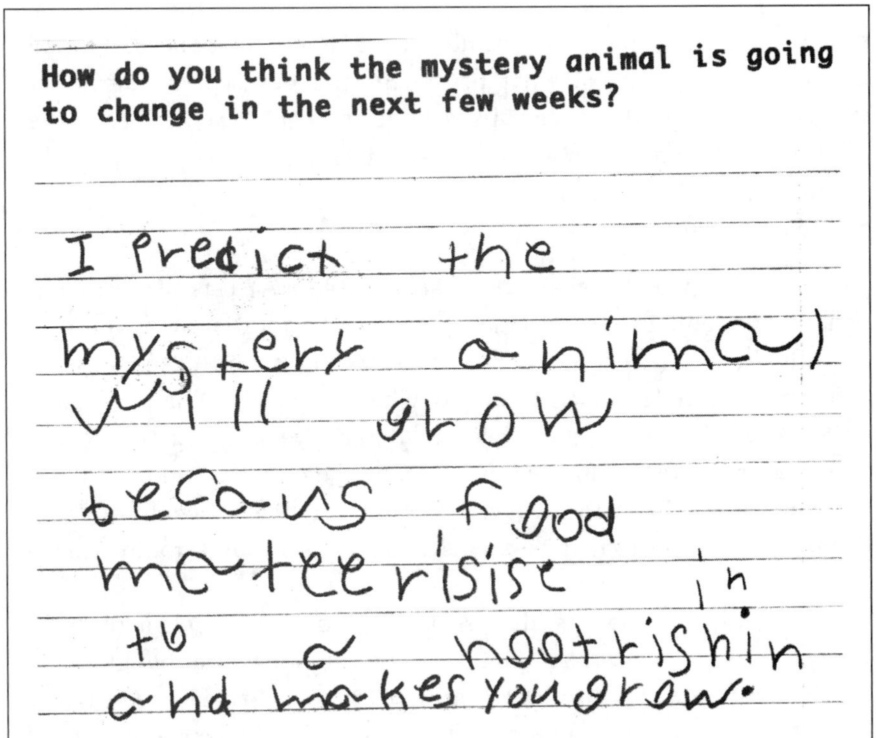

How do you think the mystery animal is going to change in the next few weeks?

I Predict the mystery animal will grow becaus food mateerisise in to a nootrishin and makes you grow.

FIGURE 5–2 Kimberly's second prediction

support their claims. Students like Kimberly typically skip right to their inferences about what they think is causing something to happen. If asked, "What makes you think that?" their answers are something like "I just know it" or "I saw it on TV." They need to learn the skill of recognizing and providing evidence for their thinking.

Components of Scientific Conclusions in the Elementary Grades

In the rest of this chapter, we will look at samples of higher-level forms of thinking and writing from students in kindergarten through fifth grade. All the children use scaffolding and strategies that prompt them to write about different components of scientific conclusions, including statements that:

- answer a question, either in a general or specific way
- provide evidence in the form of *qualitative* data (expressed in *comparative* language such as *more* or *less*; *longer* or *shorter*)
- provide evidence in the form of *quantitative* data (presented as actual *measured* data)
- express conclusions in concluding statements that are based on these data.

Depending on the investigation as well as the language skills of the students, these more complex scientific entries also might include:

- references to their prediction and whether or not their data supported it
- an inference regarding what the students think caused the outcomes
- comments regarding inconclusive or inconsistent data they had in their test results and what might have caused them (for example, uncontrolled variables)
- other questions they want to investigate.

Figure 5–3 (which is also included in Appendix A), lists all these components of a complex conclusion, which would be appropriate for fourth and fifth graders. It includes an example for each component so that students can get a better understanding of what they need to think about and write. Depending on the grade level and the science unit, you can provide your students with a form like this to remind them of what they need to be thinking and writing. Other less complex examples are shown throughout the next sections for primary students, and for specific units for intermediate students.

In small-group and class discussions, regardless of the elementary grade level, students will *talk* about *all* these components, although the terminology and sophistication of the thinking will vary. The specific components they will include in their notebook entries will depend on the students' developmental levels in writing and the focus of the particular entry.

Components of a Scientific Conclusion

- *Answer the investigative question in a general way*, using the words from the question in your answer if possible: What happens to the brightness of a bulb when you change the length of wire in a closed circuit? "When I change the length of wire in a closed circuit, the brightness of the bulb changes."
- *Provide evidence from your observations or tests. Include:*

  Qualitative data (for example, *more/less; longer/shorter; brighter/dimmer*): "The bulb was brighter with shorter wire and dimmer with longer wire."

  Quantitative data (measured data): "For example, with 10 cm wire, the bulb brightness was 9. But with the 30 cm wire, the brightness was only 7."

- *Make a concluding statement(s) that is based on the evidence*: "Therefore, the shortest wire makes the bulb the brightest and the longest wire makes the bulb the dimmest."
- *Refer to your prediction.* Did your data support it? If they did not, how has your thinking changed? "The data did not support my prediction because I thought that the bulbs would have the same brightness. I didn't think the length of the wire would make any difference. Now I know that the length does have an effect."
- *Make an inference about what you think caused these test results*: "I think this happens because longer wire has more resistance than shorter wire."
- *If you had data that were different from what other groups had, what do you think could have caused these results?* "I think my group got different results because we used a different type of wire than the others did. We should have kept that variable the same as everyone else."
- *What other questions do you have now that you want to investigate?* "What would happen if we used wires of different thicknesses?"

FIGURE 5–3 Components of a scientific conclusion

Kindergarten and First-Grade Examples

Students begin in kindergarten to learn the basics about making sense of their test results and answering questions. For example, in *Fabric*, a unit published by Full Option Science System (FOSS), kindergartners conduct an investigation to discover whether each fabric repels or absorbs water.

Before the investigation, students date the entry and glue in the focus question. After conducting and discussing the investigation, the class participates in a shared-writing minilesson. The teacher chooses one fabric and asks the students what they observed happening to a drop of water when they placed it on that fabric. As they tell her what they observed, she models how to draw their results. Then she tells them that they need to write the name of the fabric and the test results so that other scientists looking at the entry will know the outcome of their investigation. This establishes the idea that they are writing for an *audience of scientists* rather than their teacher, which helps them understand that they need to be clear in their scientific thinking and writing, and also that they are not writing the entry to please their teacher. The writing has a scientific purpose.

Before she writes the words, the teacher asks her students where they can find the words (in the science word bank), then she writes the fabric name and either *repels* or *absorbs* next to her drawing. At the early kindergarten level, the words *nylon* and *repels* are the report of the test results.

The teacher then asks them to help her write more about what they have observed, and models how they can use the environment as well as inventive spelling to write that part of the entry. After this shared writing, students choose a fabric and write in their notebook, including the same components of the entry—drawing of fabric, test results in single words, phrase or sentence about the outcome—that they have created as a class.

If this kind of minilesson is conducted with kindergartners in the fall, they copy the drawing and words into their notebook as they participate in the shared writing. From the beginning of the year, they learn to use the environment and inventive spelling to write their entries, and their teachers always leave parts of the entry for the students to do independently. During shared-writing minilessons later in the year, kindergartners draw and write on white boards or scratch paper during the modeling, then choose a fabric and draw and write their own entry independently in their notebook. Children who already know their letter-sound associations when they enter kindergarten benefit from moving more quickly to this independent level. The important thing to remember if you want students to learn how to write about their scientific thinking is to model how to draw and write about what they have *learned*, not what they have done; and to value the *content* of their drawings and writing rather than the neatness of the "product."

Students who need to dictate their writing still need to draw and write something independently, working at a place where they are challenged but not frustrated. Tracing their dictated words, which teachers write in yellow highlighter, helps children develop fine-motor skills for handwriting. Copying their dictated words from a sticky note into their notebook, then later reading the words to the teacher, helps children develop reading and writing skills while they also are using their own words to express their thinking in their notebook.

Koby wrote the October entry shown in Figure 5–4. He attended a Head Start Program, where he learned his letters, and now is served in the English Language Learner (ELL) Program. Most of his kindergarten classmates are ELL students who speak a variety of languages. The majority of them also are served in the free or reduced-price lunch program.

In this classroom, Koby's teacher uses numerous visual aids in her instruction and continually models both oral and written language. Because Koby has learned quickly from the modeling and knows how to use the environment and inventive spelling to spell the words, he is able to report quite a lot about the results of this investigation. He chooses, then copies, the words *repels*, *nylon*, and *water* from the science word bank. Then he independently writes his own sentence that describes the observed test

FIGURE 5–4 Koby's October entry

results, sounding out the words that he does not know or cannot find in the classroom.

In March, Koby has progressed to making more complex entries, including providing reasoning in his writing. The class is studying a second science unit (*Animals Two by Two*, another unit published by FOSS) and is planning an investigation to test what foods snails seem to eat. (This is a supplemental lesson that the school district's science program has added to the unit to meet state standards and to provide more inquiry-based experiences for kindergartners. The question has been changed to "What foods do land snails eat?" The word *prefer* humanizes the snail's behavior.)

The teacher models how to make a box table, adding simple illustrations and names of the foods the class has chosen to test. The kindergartners make the table in their notebook (see Koby's table in Figure 5–5), adding the details as the class discusses what to include in the data table. The illustrations help the ELL students, as well as nonreaders, identify and learn the written words in the table. Students then conduct the tests in small groups, recording a tally mark in the data table in their notebook as the snail goes to each food. (Koby's group did numerous tests with their snail.) After the class discusses the results of each group's investigation, the teacher models in a shared writing how students can write about their conclusions.

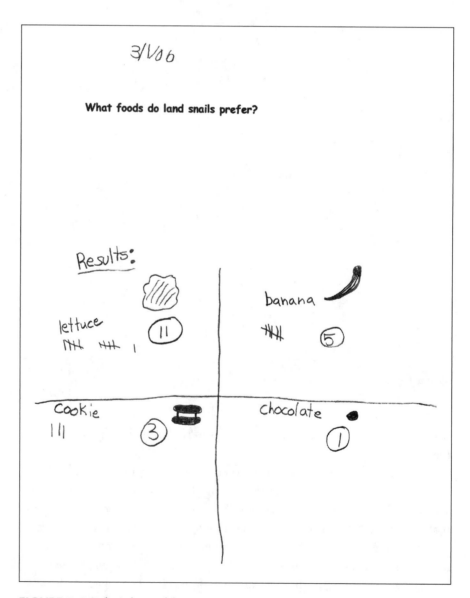

FIGURE 5–5 Koby's box table

In Figure 5–6, Koby reports his conclusion based on the data in his table: "Land snails prefer lettuce." Then he adds his inferential thinking, which was not prompted: "because he is a plant eater and they like it because they like plants." The class has been reading about herbivores and carnivores, and he is using his knowledge to infer that the reason snails eat lettuce is that they are plant eaters. He has learned to use *because* to introduce his reasoning. In a discussion with the student, his teacher would ask about what he *observed* that makes him think that his land snail prefers lettuce. This would prompt him to provide *quantitative data* to support his thinking: "I think the land snail prefers lettuce because it went to the lettuce 11 times. That is lots more times than for the other food." Having provided evidence, then he could infer that land snails are plant eaters.

This is another example of the benefits and pitfalls of using the word *because*. In teaching students how to use the word in reporting test results, it is important to distinguish between what they actually *observe* and what they *think* or *infer* is causing the outcome.

As early as kindergarten, children can learn through discussion and modeling to provide such evidence and inferences in their speaking and writing. Small-group and class discussions are essential in teaching students not only the need to provide evidence for their thinking but also the language they can use in doing so. For instance, "What is your evidence?" is a common question—even from classmates—to ask during such discussions. Students then learn such responses as "My evidence is" or "My data are," which help them state their observations and/or quantitative (measured) data. As mentioned earlier, the scientific skills of providing evidence, especially for inferential reasoning, can be particularly challenging for students with highly developed thinking and language abilities, so they benefit from this modeling as well.

Figure 5–7 is an entry written by Munira, an ELL first grader with weak but developing skills in English. (She repeated first grade the next year.) The class has conducted an investigation to explore how the height of a ramp—either one block or two blocks high—affects how a ball rolls and moves an object (a block) at the bottom of the ramp. (This is an investigation in *Balls and Ramps*, a unit published by Insights.) The student has learned through discussion and shared-writing minilessons to answer the question, then support her answer with quantitative data.

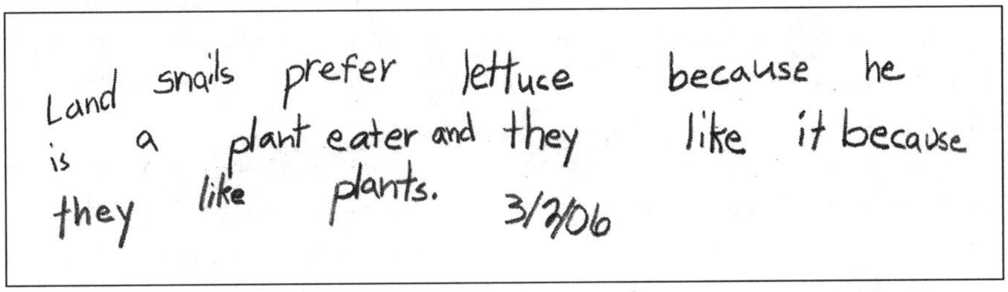

Land snails prefer lettuce because he is a plant eater and they like it because they like plants. 3/7/06

FIGURE 5–6 Koby's conclusion

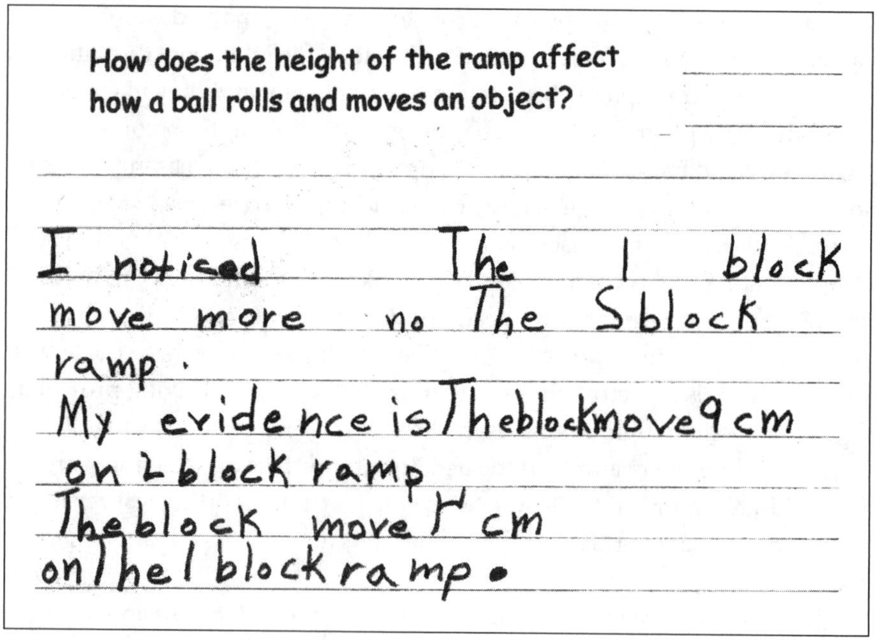

How does the height of the ramp affect how a ball rolls and moves an object?

I noticed The 1 block move more no The 5 block ramp.

My evidence is Theblockmove 9 cm on 2 block ramp The block move 1 cm on the 1 block ramp.

FIGURE 5–7 Munira's entry

The phrases "I noticed" and "My evidence is" are part of the classroom's "scientific language." All the children—about 25 percent are in the ELL program and 75 percent are in the free or reduced-price lunch program—routinely use this language and understand that they need to provide evidence for their thinking. In this case, they know they must report the results of the tests from *both* ramps in order to provide evidence for what effect the angle of the ramp has on the balls. Typically, students in elementary school will not provide enough data from their tests in their writing. In this entry, Munira provides both the general answer—"I noticed the 1 block move more no [on] the 2 block ramp"—and the quantitative data from both ramps to support her first statement. She has learned to do this during classroom science discussions and the teacher's oral and written modeling of the language.

Jason, one of Munira's classmates, wrote the entry shown in Figure 5–8. Jason also is served in the ELL program but has developed more skills in English at this point than Munira has. He makes a data table and then records the data from his group's investigation. In a class discussion about quantitative data, students learn to circle the number in the middle or the number that occurs most often in a column of data, and to cross out the other number or numbers.

Jason answers the question, then provides quantitative data for both the one-block and two-block ramps. But because of his stronger skills and his teacher's ongoing modeling of such talking and writing, he then provides his inferential thinking about why he thinks the block moved farther in one case than the other. The class uses the phrase "I think" to distinguish

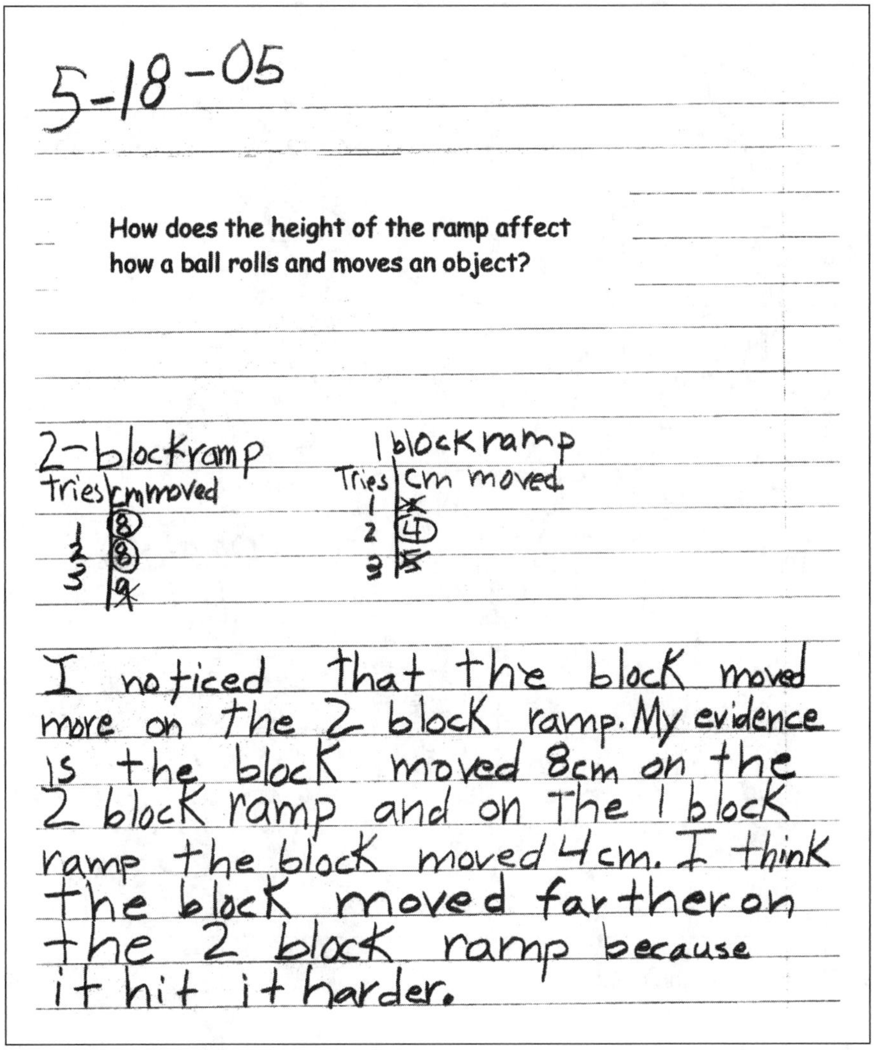

FIGURE 5–8 Jason's data and conclusion

answers that are inferences. Here he is inferring that the block moved farther when the ball coming down the two-block ramp hit it because that ball hit it harder than the ball from the one-block ramp did. He is expressing an initial idea about momentum, a concept that he will not be able to understand until his abstract thinking begins to develop, but his teacher constantly encourages students to describe their observations and then what they infer from them.

JuJuan, a first grader in another class, wrote the entry in Figure 5–9, which includes more components of a complex answer. In an extension of one of the learning experiences in the *Balls and Ramps* unit, students test different balls to see which ones bounce better. After a class discussion about the results of their investigations and a shared-writing minilesson, the teacher gives the students the sentence starter "A good bouncer _____ ." Students are to provide their class definition of a good

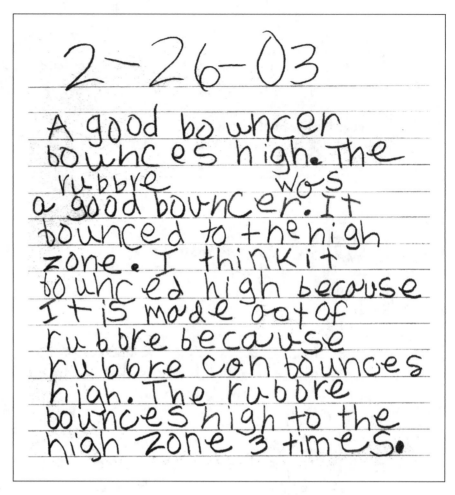

FIGURE 5–9 JuJuan's entry

bouncer (it bounces high rather than a number of times or for a long period of time). Then they are to present their evidence from the investigation and explain why they think or infer one ball is a better bouncer than another.

JuJuan begins his entry by finishing the sentence starter with the students' operational definition of a good bouncer: "A good bouncer bounces high." Then he provides the general results of his group's tests: "The rubbre [ball] was a good bouncer." He supports the statement with qualitative data: "It bounced to the high zone." (The teacher has vertically arranged three "zones" of different colors of paper on a blank wall. This is where they test to see how high each ball bounces. The green paper or "zone" is the highest.)

Next, JuJuan adds his inferences, which are based on earlier experiences with rubber balls. Again, the phrase "I think" is what many students in this class have learned to use to begin their oral and written inferences, which they know they must support by adding *because* and their reasoning. He concludes with additional data to support the validity of his test results: "The rubbre bounces high to the high zone 3 times." In class discussions, students have learned that they need to conduct a test at least three times (at the elementary level) before they can think that their results are valid. Although this final sentence should be combined with the third sentence in this entry, science notebook entries are by nature rough drafts, so this is a minor issue, especially given all the strong components he has included.

Second- and Third-Grade Examples

In the late primary and early intermediate grades, students can have difficulty with another complex type of entry in which they must identify something and justify the identification with their observations and test results. In *Soils*, a unit published by STC, second graders learn how to observe different properties of soil and conduct tests to discover additional properties. They record their observations and test results in tables.

At the end of the unit, students use their scientific skills to observe a sample of the local soil and conduct several different tests to determine which soil components—sand, clay, and/or humus—are in the local soil. This is a complex process, and one that is equally difficult to write about. However, if students—both in discussions and in their writing—learn how to make good observations and conduct tests well, record their results accurately, and use their tables as thinking and prewriting organizers (as described in Chapter 4), they will be able to provide organized and thorough reasoning for the identification.

This particular identification process includes a test to determine if the soil sample can roll into a ball (the "ball test"), how it settles in a tube of water (the "settling test"), what happens when it is smeared on a piece of paper (the "smear test"), and how much water the soil holds when water is poured on it (the "draining test").

In Figure 5–10, Madeline, who is in second grade, writes about the soil components she thinks are in the local soil. She has above-average language skills, and uses her tables, and thus the tests, as the prewriting organizer, as modeled throughout the unit by her teacher. The phrase "When I did" helps her introduce the results of each test. The words "like the" help her connect these test results with the results of previous tests. If she were older, she might write, "When I did the ball test, the soil did not make a ball, which was what the humus did in the earlier investigation." "Like the humus" is a kind of shorthand wording that supplies that same information. She has learned certain phrases such as "in addition" in shared-writing minilessons. The rest of the language in the entry is her own, as are the detailed observations and test results.

Articulating a process of identification becomes a little more complex in third grade. In *Rocks and Minerals*, a unit published by STC, students work with twelve minerals and learn how to observe them and conduct various tests to determine the properties of the minerals. In a summative assessment at the end of the unit, students use their new scientific skills to identify three "mystery minerals." For this entry, the teacher models, in a shared-writing minilesson, how to include the properties and test results in

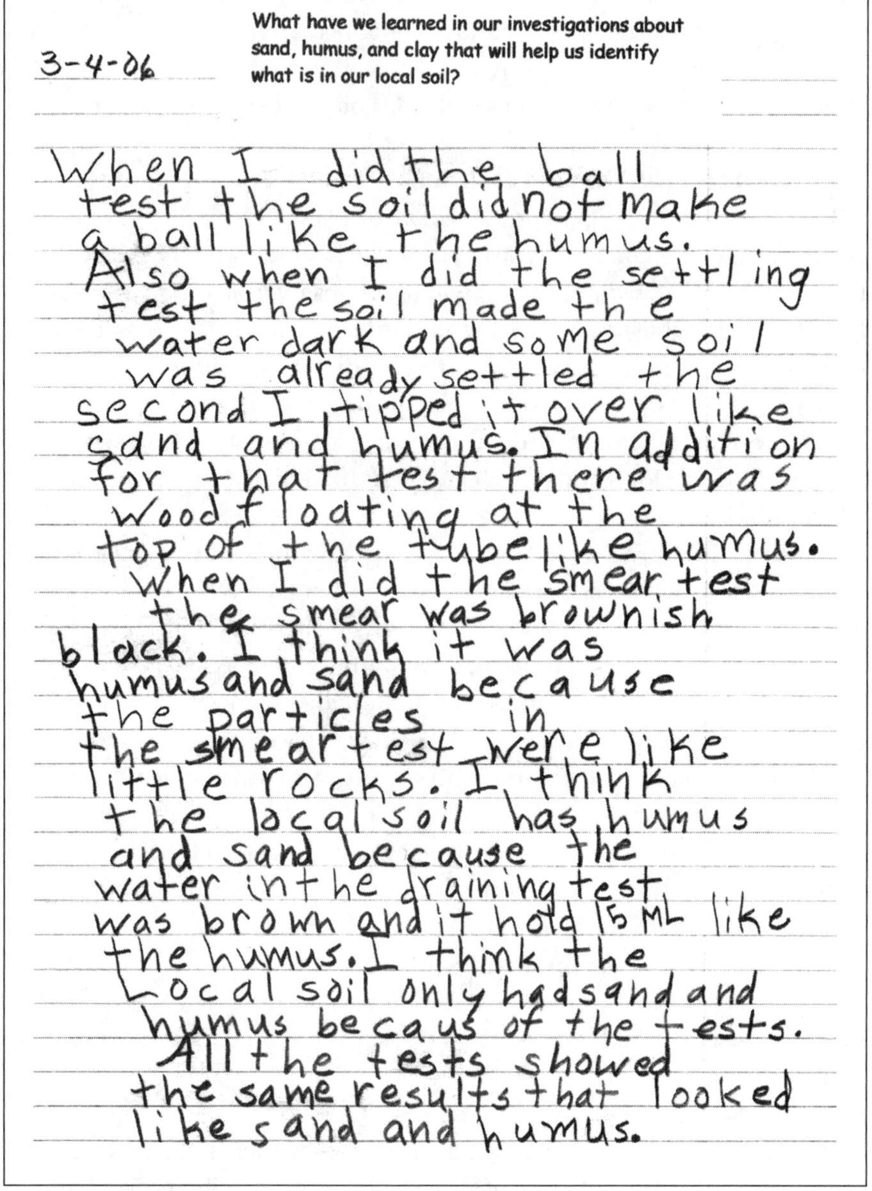

> **3-4-06**
>
> **What have we learned in our investigations about sand, humus, and clay that will help us identify what is in our local soil?**
>
> When I did the ball test the soil did not make a ball like the humus. Also when I did the settling test the soil made the water dark and some soil was already settled the second I tipped it over like sand and humus. In addition for that test there was wood floating at the top of the tube like humus. When I did the smear test the smear was brownish black. I think it was humus and sand because the particles in the smear test were like little rocks. I think the local soil has humus and sand because the water in the draining test was brown and it hold 15 ML like the humus. I think the Local soil only had sand and humus becaus of the tests. All the tests showed the same results that looked like sand and humus.

FIGURE 5–10 Madeline's identification of soils

the process of identifying a mystery mineral. (She does her modeling with a mineral that her students will not be identifying.) To support students in making their own notebook entry, she provides a topic sentence starter for each paragraph.

The sample in Figure 5–11 was written by Julienny, an ELL student whose skills in writing are somewhat low—she struggles with generating ideas and details as well as writing fluent sentences. But because of the sentence starters, writing frames, and other language forms she has learned, she is beginning to be successful midway through the year in her expository writing in science as well as in math.

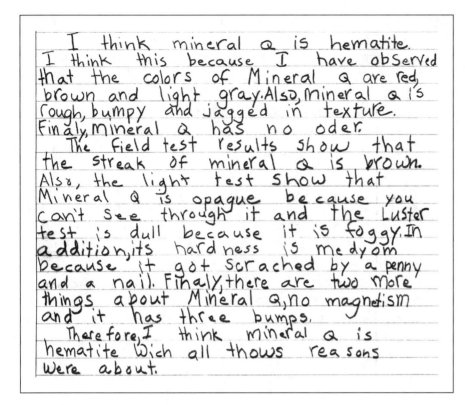

I think mineral Q is hematite.
I think this because I have observed
that the colors of Mineral Q are red,
brown and light gray. Also, mineral Q is
rough, bumpy and jagged in texture.
Finaly, mineral Q has no oder.
The field test results show that
the streak of mineral Q is brown.
Also, the light test show that
Mineral Q is opaque because you
can't see through it and the Luster
test is dull because it is foggy. In
addition, its hardness is medyom
because it got scrached by a penny
and a nail. Finaly, there are two more
things about Mineral Q, no magnetism
and it has three bumps.
Therefore, I think mineral Q is
hematite wich all thows reasons
were about.

FIGURE 5–11 Julienny's identification of a mineral

Throughout the unit, her teacher has modeled how to write about observations and test results, so Julienny is comfortable by the end of the unit with providing details of her observations and test results. The scaffolding of the simple sentence starters also helps her write an organized, detailed entry using the evidence she has collected.

The first sentence starter in the entry—"I think Mineral Q is _____"—helps her begin. (Facing a blank page is daunting for many students, and sentence starters help provide some momentum.) Julienny knows that she can provide evidence with the sentence starter "I think this because." She introduces her observations with "I observed," and begins with them because she made observations before she began conducting the tests on the "mystery mineral." Throughout the year, she has been learning different transition words such as *also* and *finally*, which she uses independently throughout this entry.

In the second paragraph, she explains the results of some of the tests, again without prompting. For example, rather than simply writing, "The light test shows that Mineral Q is opaque," she elaborates by adding "because you can't see through it." The teacher has modeled this kind of thinking and language in class discussions about each of the tests. Julienny clearly has benefited from the repetition of the oral and written modeling.

Students with more developed language skills could be more discriminating by focusing first on the distinctive properties of the mineral that distinguish it as hematite, rather than listing every property in order. But this more structured approach supports students like Julienny, who are developing language skills. The strategy also helps students who rather randomly include evidence in their thinking and writing.

Fourth- and Fifth-Grade Examples

As the science content and the science units themselves become more complex in the intermediate elementary grades, students need to learn to provide more detailed evidence and explain more complex thinking in their notebook entries. This is especially true, of course, in their analysis of data and conclusions. As mentioned at the beginning of this chapter, a conclusion includes (not necessarily in the following order) a general answer, qualitative and/or quantitative data that explain and support the answer, and concluding statements. In some cases, concluding entries for investigations may also include inferences, comments about inconclusive or inconsistent data, references to a prediction, and new questions. Learning such skills is considerably easier for students if, in the class discussions and shared-writing minilessons, teachers explicitly address these components, including discussions of data.

After a class discussion of the results of an investigation that includes quantitative (measured) data, a wall chart of the Data Analysis frame in Figure 5–12 can help scaffold conclusions in a class discussion as well as during a shared-writing minilesson about how to write about data in a graph. (This frame is also helpful for writing about data in mathematics. A more detailed blackline master is included in Appendix A.) Most students benefit from beginning with scaffolding like this before they move into independent expression of such thinking. However, it is extremely important for all students to realize that scaffolding—like training wheels on bicycles—are there to support students only as they are learning basic skills. After a while, children can move away from the support and write in various ways using different language while still including the same fundamental elements.

A class of fourth graders and their teacher found the Data Analysis frame helpful in discussing and writing about the results of an investigation they had conducted from the unit *Magnetism and Electricity*, published by FOSS. The class had been testing how the number of spacers placed between two magnets affects the number of washers the magnets can hold. Rather than using the bar graph blackline master in the unit, the teacher guided the students in creating their own graph, as her student Connor did in his notebook entry shown in Figure 5–13. (This process is discussed in the making tables section of Chapter 4.) In this way, students learn how to take data from their table and create an appropriate graph as a visual representation or "story" of their test results. The students learn how to graph the changed or manipulated variable (the number of spacers, in this case) on the *x*-axis, and the measured or responding variable (the number of

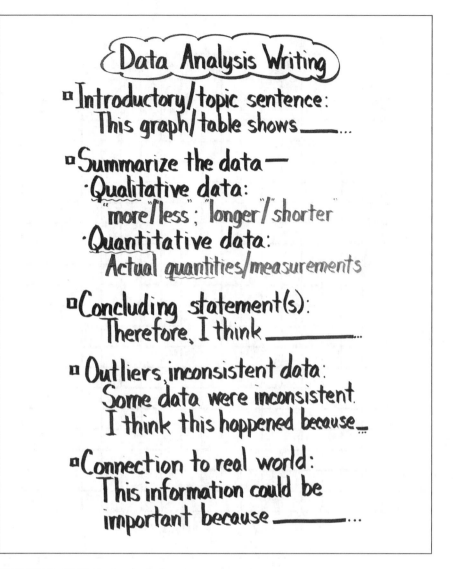

FIGURE 5–12 Data Analysis frame

washers the magnets hold) on the *y*-axis. As they discuss the data in a graph that they have created themselves, they begin to develop deeper understanding of the results of their investigation as well as words they can use to communicate their understanding. They then use the graph as a prewriting organizer for their conclusion.

Connor, who has strong skills for a fourth grader, wrote a conclusion, shown in Figure 5–14, to the question that the students have been investigating: "How does the number of spacers affect the force of attraction between two magnets?" He begins his conclusion with a general, *qualitative* answer: "When we put *more spacers* between the magnets it took *less washers* to break the force." Next, he supports the statement with his "proof," which includes both ends of the range of data as well as the data point (one spacer) that shows the greatest change. His concluding statement is a

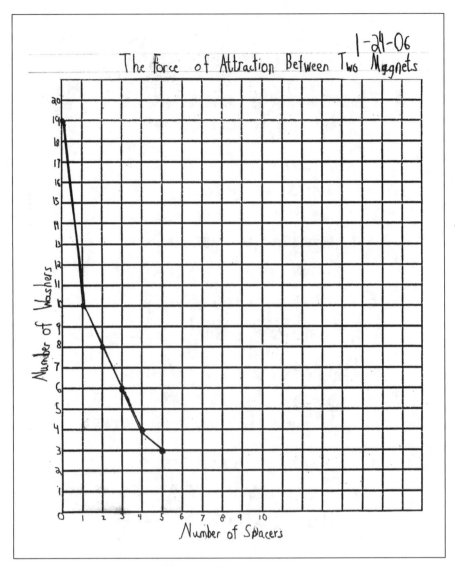

FIGURE 5–13 Connor's test results

reasonable inference based on his data. Then he ends with a question, which he could investigate in another experiment.

Interestingly, the afternoon before Connor and his classmates wrote their conclusions, their teacher participated in one of the fourth-grade writing workshops in Seattle's Science Notebooks Program. The program facilitator and a group of fourth-grade teachers discussed data analysis and how to help students learn how to write about data in their conclusions, in part by using the Data Analysis frame. Connor's teacher then applied what she had learned as she planned her instruction for the next day. Her students' notebook entries were remarkably strong, and convinced her of the benefits of using the discussion strategies and this particular frame.

The more complex conclusions shown in the next three notebook entries are from fifth-grade classmates with varying language skills. They

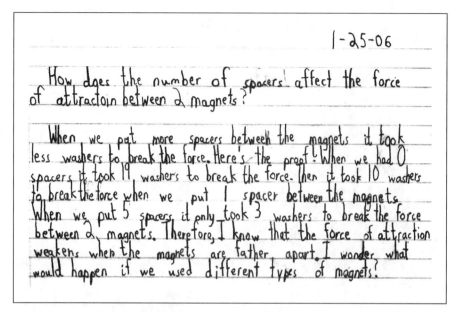

1-25-06

How does the number of spacers affect the force of attractoin between 2 magnets?

When we put more spacers between the magnets it took less washers to break the force. Here's the proof! When we had 0 spacers it took 19 washers to break the force. Then it took 10 washers to break the force when we put 1 spacer between the magnets. When we put 5 spacers, it only took 3 washers to break the force between 2 magnets. Therefore, I know that the force of attraction weakens when the magnets are father apart. I wonder what would happen if we used different types of magnets?

FIGURE 5–14 Connor's conclusion

attend a Seattle public school in which over 75 percent of the school's students receive free or reduced-price lunch and almost 50 percent have limited English proficiency. The fifth graders have been studying *Models and Designs*, a unit published by FOSS. The elementary science program staff has developed a lesson in which students design their own investigations using standardized go-carts. In this case, the students have decided to investigate the question "How does wheel size affect the distance a go-cart can travel?" They have used a planning template (shown in Figure 3–6 in Chapter 3 and Appendix A) to set up their investigations, conducted the trials in small groups, discussed their data together as a class, created a class graph that includes each group's data, and discussed their results.

The teacher then leads a shared-writing minilesson to model how to write conclusions to their investigations. As has been her practice throughout the year in class discussions and shared-writing minilessons, the teacher models the necessary language both orally and in writing, holding up words from the word bank as needed, and teaches the children—many of whom are ELL students—how to use scientific language. During part of the discussion, she writes on the white board what students say (see Figure 5–15), modeling how to reword the sentence if necessary to express the idea in various—and sometimes more sophisticated or scientific—ways without making any student feel that his comment is not valuable and articulate.

As students continue to contribute their ideas about the data, she models how to rephrase their thoughts into such statements as "The *larger* wheels make the go-carts travel *farther* than the *smaller* wheels do." Later on, when students are ready to make generalizations about the results, she models how to make their statements into a generalization such as, "I think

FIGURE 5–15 Teacher models how to rephrase sentences

this means that the larger the wheel, the farther a go-cart will travel." Once the discussion gets to this point, the students can consider whether they think that this generalization would always be true, then discuss what they might do to test this broader generalization.

After extensive discussion in small groups and as a class, students write their own conclusions. Most of them use, to varying degrees, a writing frame that the teacher gives to them. For a conclusion to an investigation that has fairly simple quantitative data, the frame might look like this:

I think _____ [General answer to the investigative question]. I think this because _____ [Quantitative evidence]. Therefore, _____ [More specific answer to the investigative question].

The data show my prediction was _____ [Answer to these two questions: Did your data support your prediction? How has your thinking changed, if it has?].

Some data were inconclusive. I think this happened because _____ [Answer this question: If you had inconclusive data, what do you think caused that to happen?].

The teacher also shows students how to use their data table as a prewriting organizer so that they will remember to include the important quantitative data. By this time in the unit, which the class is studying in the fall, many students have learned the language in the frame and understand what they need to include in their conclusions. They also choose whether they want to use the data from their small-group tests or from the class data, which all the groups have collected and combined in a class graph.

The three samples in Figures 5–16, 5–17, and 5–18 illustrate how the frame helps students at various stages of language and writing development write conclusions. Lisa, the student whose entry is shown in Figure 5–16, has strong language skills and has qualified for the district's gifted program for the sixth grade. Remembering that these notebook entries are always rough drafts, note that she begins by stating an answer to the investigative question. "I think this because" introduces the quantitative data that support her first statement. She then provides the qualitative supporting data ("The medium wheel size travels farther than the small wheel size" and so on). She also makes a copy of her graph to provide a visual representation of her data—which she further supports with the caption "The line goes up."

Lisa's concluding statement answers the question with slightly different wording, then she addresses her prediction. Interestingly, earlier in her notebook, she predicts that the smaller wheels will go farther because they are lighter. She does not refer back to that prediction, possibly because she does not want to admit to being "wrong." This is a common issue with students of all ages, but if the classroom culture values inquiry, students begin to understand that scientists learn as much from when their investigation results are not what they expected as they do when the prediction is "right." Referring back to a prediction also helps students think about what they have learned from their investigation.

Lisa's entry includes all the major components of a complete conclusion to an investigation. She presumably does not address the issue of inconclusive or inconsistent data because her group did not have such data. Her

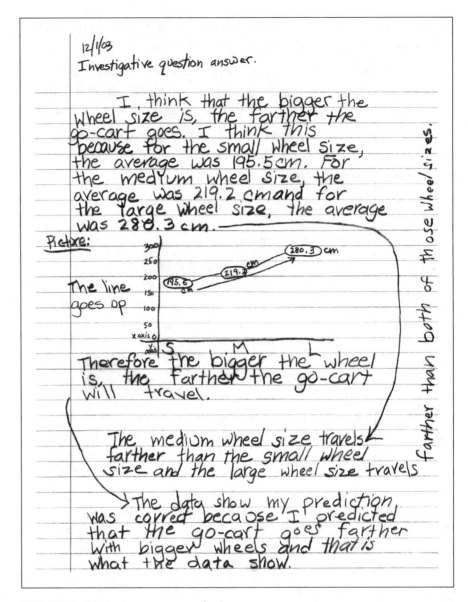

The handwritten journal entry reads:

12/1/03
Investigative question answer.

I think that the bigger the wheel size is, the farther the go-cart goes. I think this because for the small wheel size, the average was 195.5 cm. For the medium wheel size, the average was 219.2 cm and for the large wheel size, the average was 288.3 cm.

Picture:

The line goes up

Therefore the bigger the wheel is, the farther the go-cart will travel.

The medium wheel size travels farther than the small wheel size and the large wheel size travels

The data show my prediction was correct because I predicted that the go-cart goes farther with bigger wheels and that is what the data show.

farther than both of those wheel sizes.

FIGURE 5–16 Lisa's go-cart conclusion

entry could have included additional scientific thinking if she had written about why the larger wheels might travel farther than wheels of a smaller diameter.

The entry illustrates a common problem with elementary students: She has included all the data rather than *summarizing* it. She does not need to write about the middle wheels. This does not cause a significant problem in this case, but students typically write about every data point in a graph. In class discussions and shared-writing minilessons, teach them how to report data from the lowest and highest points in the range that are not outliers.

My Na, who wrote the conclusion in Figure 5–17, is a bright, conscientious student who is served in the ELL program. She understands and can use much of the language correctly and independently, but she diligently

12/1/03 Standard Go-Cart Writing

I think the bigger the wheels are, the farther our go-cart travels ^on the rug because as the wheels get bigger, it gains even more energy to the wheels, which makes it push itself, ^when cranking it and setting it down and will travel farther. Also, my data's averages on mine go farther in small wheels, more farther for medium wheels, and a little bit more farther in large wheels than medium wheels. My data says the average my go-cart traveled for small wheels were 206.6cm. Medium wheels are 306.6 cm, and for large wheels, it is 327cm of the average. Therefore, the big wheels went farther than the other wheel sizes.

My prediction of thinking that small wheels would go farther was incorrect because testing the small wheel size three times, adding it all together and dividing by three makes 206.6 cm. The other wheel size's (not including the hubs) averages were bigger than the small wheel average. All of my averages fit with the other data, which tells me I don't have any inconclusive results in my data.

In conclusion, wheel size affects the distance a go-cart can travel by how big the wheel sizes get. The bigger your wheel size is, the farther it travels and gains more energy to push itself. For example, when cranking it up, and setting it down, it's like when you see it go on the rug, it's like it's pushing itself all the way with all it's energy, till it can't go any farther no more.

FIGURE 5–17 My Na's conclusion

follows the frame to remind herself of what to include. She also writes about more than the frame indicates. In her opening statement, she makes some inferences, based on her prior investigations with go-carts and her thoughts about energy. She then presents her qualitative data about the different wheel sizes, each one going *farther* (qualitative or comparative data) than the smaller one. Next, she provides the quantitative data from her group's trials. Note that she, too, does not summarize the data. She then deals with her prediction and makes her case for why her group's data are not inconclusive. (Because she is comparing her group's data with the class results, and her data match the trend or pattern of class data, she should write that her data are *consistent*—or not inconsistent—with the cumulative results.)

As she writes her concluding paragraph, she again includes her inference regarding why she thinks the largest wheels make the go-cart travel the farthest distance. Students often mix up their inferential thinking with their concluding statements. To help them write stronger conclusions, teach them how to present their data first, then write a conclusion to the investigative question. Then they can write their inferences about what might be causing the results.

Complex conclusions also often reveal misconceptions. In this case, My Na is confused about energy. Regardless of the size of the wheels, each go-cart has the same amount of stored or potential energy because the students have controlled this variable by using the same number of twists of the same types of rubber bands on the axles. To help reexamine her inferential thinking, she could observe the go-cart more carefully, considering, for example, how far a go-cart moves with one rotation of its axle depending on the circumference of the wheels. This will help her deal with her misconception about energy.

Flor, who wrote the conclusion in Figure 5–18, is another ELL student who is bright but not so dedicated a student as the other two. The frame helps her address most of the components of the conclusion, which she otherwise might not include. She does not answer the question about how her thinking has changed given that the data do not support her prediction. This could lead her to think and write about some inferences regarding why the larger wheels cause the go-cart to travel a longer distance.

She also includes details about why she considers some of her group's data to be "inconclusive." This may be the most interesting, or perhaps the most frustrating, part of the investigation for her at this point. Investigations like this frequently result in *inconclusive* data—test results that do not show a clear pattern that supports a definite conclusion—because students cannot control all variables. Even though Flor's group tries to control everything in an investigation, the go-cart does not behave in approximately the same way each time the students run the same test, so they cannot reach a conclusion. However, when all the groups contribute data to the class graph of data, the *class* results are conclusive—they clearly support the

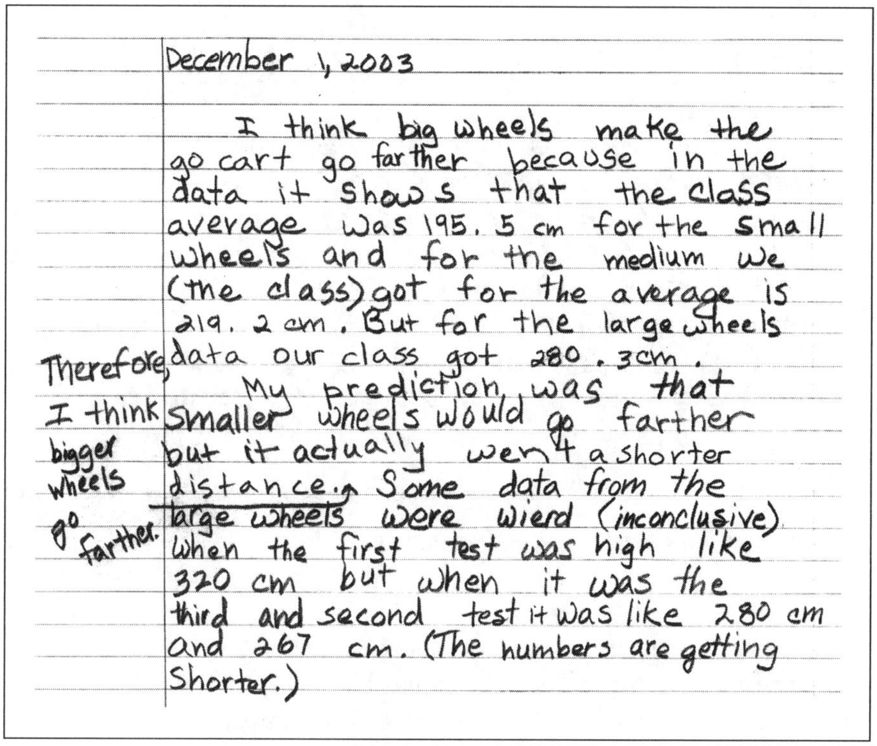

December 1, 2003

I think big wheels make the go cart go farther because in the data it shows that the class average was 195.5 cm for the small wheels and for the medium we (the class) got for the average is 219.2 cm. But for the large wheels data our class got 280.3cm.

Therefore, I think bigger wheels go farther. My prediction was that smaller wheels would go farther but it actually went a shorter distance. Some data from the large wheels were wierd (inconclusive) when the first test was high like 320 cm but when it was the third and second test it was like 280 cm and 267 cm. (The numbers are getting shorter.)

FIGURE 5–18 Flor's concluding entry

same conclusion. So now Flor's group data are *inconsistent* with that of the pattern made by the data from all the groups. An important, but frustrating, lesson for students is that scientific investigations do not always result in conclusive data.

In a relatively short time, many students can learn to write conclusions like Flor, My Na, and Lisa have written when the investigations result in quantitative data. But most students have greater difficulty writing conclusions that have only qualitative data, or a combination of both qualitative and quantitative evidence. A simple example is shown in Anna's entry in Figure 5–19. Her fifth-grade class has been studying *Microworlds*, a unit published by STC, and the students have conducted an investigation in which they have discovered that to be a magnifier, an object must be convex and transparent. Their next investigation (a lesson that the science program staff has developed to meet state science standards) is designed to answer the question "How does the shape of a water drop affect how much it will magnify?" In pairs, students put a drop of water on a square of waxed paper, which they then place over letters on a piece of newspaper. They are to observe both the shape of the drop and the degree of magnification of the letters. Students then add drops to the first water drop so the original drop contains three, then five, then ten, and finally thirteen drops. Students observe and record the shape of the drop and its magnification each time they add more water.

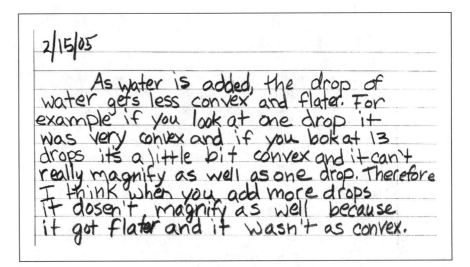

FIGURE 5–19 Anna's simple conclusion

To write the conclusion, students know that they are to begin with a general answer to the question, then support it with specific evidence. "For example" is a typical phrase that students in this class use in introducing their evidence. Because there are no measured or quantitative data, students can report only qualitative data about their observations. They use the data table they have made in their notebook as their organizer. Anna remembers to summarize rather than regurgitate all the data, perhaps because the groups have tested so many versions of the changed variable in this investigation that she does not want to include all the data. (The test results with the go-carts include only three wheels, so students might not understand the need to *summarize* that data.) "Therefore, I think" is a phrase that many students use in stating their concluding thoughts. Because of this structure, and the investigation itself, this student is able to write a concise and complete conclusion.

This becomes more challenging with more complicated investigations. In Figure 5–20, Anna J., a fourth grader, writes a complex conclusion for a long-term investigation that she and her classmates have conducted based on the *Ecosystems* unit, published by STC. Each team of students has written an investigative question regarding what effect a given pollutant might have on their terrarium and aquarium. Because students have removed animals from the habitats so that the organisms will not die, students also are to consider what they think might happen to animals based on what students observe happening to the plants over time. The teams have planned their investigations, then conducted them over a period of weeks, collecting and recording both qualitative data (observations of the different plants, for instance) and quantitative data (measurements of the pH) from the aquariums and terrariums. (Students refer to these as *models* because they represent, but are not the same as, real ecosystems.)

> 1/7/05
>
> The queition we tride to answer
> was how does salt affect the model
> terrarium and aquarium? Many changes
> over time, for example in the terrarium
> the grass was light green and very tall.
> But then at the bottom of the grass
> it ternd brown and it clumped to one side.
> Also the alfalfa was light green but
> then after the third time we polluted
> the alfalfa is dead. Another change we
> obsverd the ph scale in the terrarium
> was 8 but then at the end the ph scale
> is 5. Knowing what happened to the
> animals and plants in the polluted terrarium,
> I think the animals would die
> because if the plants died the animals
> wouldn't have enough food.
>   The changes in the Aquarium are
> that the water was clear but at
> the end the water is yellow. The Ph
> Scale was 7 1/2 when we started then
> at the end the ph scale is 5. Also
> the Aqarium have not changed a lot.
>   I think if we put the cloudfish
> and snails in to the pollutied
> Aquarium I think the animals would
> live a little longer.
>   My answer to my queition is the
> plants all died in the terrarium and
> the salt affected the aquarium by
> making the water tern yellow.

FIGURE 5–20 Anna J.'s conclusion about change over time

When all the groups have completed their experiments and everyone has discussed the results, the teacher models how the students can structure their conclusions. By this time of the year, the students know how to use their tables as organizers and have a good understanding of transition words and other language they might use. So the scaffolding the teacher provides is simple. For the topic sentence, he writes on the overhead, "The question we were trying to answer was _____ ." Then he lists "Terrarium— changes over time" and "For example" as simple reminders to include evidence. To prompt students to write about their inferences regarding how the pollutants might affect animals if they were in such environments, he writes,

"Knowing what happened to the plants in the polluted terrarium, _____ ."
He provides similar scaffolding for writing about the aquarium. The list
ends with "The answer to our question _____ ." Students can choose to use
the scaffolding if they want to, but everyone must address these components
of the investigations.

Figure 5–20 illustrates how Anna J., a child with learning challenges
involving information processing and Attention Deficit Disorder, can write
a strong conclusion to a complex investigation quite independently. She
uses the teacher's simple scaffolding and uses her tables of observations
and data as organizers as well. Having benefited from her teacher's
inquiry-science and science-writing instruction in third grade, too (he
teaches the same students in third, then fourth grade), she knows how to
set up sentences that express changes over time through contrasts, a skill
she began to learn in writing about contrasts using a T-chart (see the
"Comparisons" section in Chapter 4).

These skills are evident when Anna J. writes the following section:

> Many changes over time, for example in the terrarium the grass was
> light green and very tall. *But then* at the bottom of the grass it ternd
> brown and it clumped to one side. Also the alfalfa was light green *but
> then after the third time we polluted* the alfalfa is dead.

In the first sentence, which needs editing, she forgets to include something
that refers to "at first" or "in the beginning" to set up the contrast, and she
needs to include "after polluting" to complete her "but then" transition.
Her next sentence is clearer, although she should provide evidence to support her statement that the alfalfa is dead. Despite these editorial issues
with her writing, this student clearly has observed changes in the terrarium
since the pollutant was introduced. And she is benefiting from using scaffolding and her tables as organizers.

Her teacher has used a T-chart in class discussions to illustrate how
students can contrast how something appears *in the beginning* of an investigation with how it is *after* something has happened. This strategy helps
elementary students of all ages see the contrast as well as use the organizer
to describe the contrast in writing. Using frames such as "At first, _____ .
But now, _____ ." and "Before [polluting], _____ . After [polluting],
_____ ." helps students learn how to express changes that occur over time
as well as cause-and-effect relationships.

In the first paragraph, Anna J. also includes qualitative evidence about
the grass and alfalfa and quantitative data about the pH, all of which support her thinking that the animals would die if the plants were gone. Although she makes an error when she writes, "Knowing what happened to
the *animals* and plants" (animals are not included in the pollution investigation), notebook entries are rough drafts. She writes quite a strong first
paragraph, especially considering the learning challenges she has.

Anna J. includes the same kinds of strong evidence in her second paragraph, but since her evidence does not indicate dramatic effects from the pollutant, she reasons that the animals probably would live longer there than in the terrarium. Her final statement clearly states her conclusion to the investigation.

Another student might have added more inferential thinking or further questions to investigate, but this entry includes the basic components of a good conclusion. Anna J. provides both qualitative and quantitative evidence about the terrarium and aquarium before and after they are polluted. Students often will provide only one type of evidence (just the quantitative data, for example, or just the qualitative data when both types of data are available). Or they will discuss the test results for the end of the investigation without contrasting them with the measured and observed variables at the beginning of the investigation (in this case the pH and the plants in the terrarium, for instance). The "but then" structure helps students remember to include the "before-and-after data"; the data tables help them remember to include a variety of observed and measured variables (in this investigation, for example, the alfalfa, grass, and pH in the terrarium; the water and pH in the aquarium); and the teacher's simple scaffolding provides general reminders about the basic content of this complex entry.

The final sample in this chapter (shown in Figure 5–21) illustrates how Calvin, a fifth grader, approached writing a very complex conclusion to an investigation in the *Land and Water* unit, published by STC. Several times in this unit, students conduct an investigation about erosion and deposition of land in a tub called a *stream table* (shown in Figure 4–3 in Chapter 4). Students pour water into a cup (the *source* of this "stream"), which is attached above one end of the stream table. In the "Basic Stream" investigation, the cup has a hole through which the water flows onto the soil, then over and through the soil to the opposite end of the stream table, then out a drainage hole into a "dump bucket." In the "Rushing River" investigation, the cup has a larger hole, which causes greater and faster water flow and subsequently more erosion and deposition than in the "Basic Stream" investigation. Finally, in the "Steep Slope" investigation, the students place a book under the end of the tub that has the cup (the same one they used in the previous investigation). This creates a steep slope, which causes the water to flow much faster than in the previous investigations, thus creating much more erosion and deposition.

After this "Steep Slope" investigation, students write a conclusion to the investigative question, "How does sloped land affect the flow of water and the amount of erosion and deposition?" To write a response to this question, students need to know how to describe many different sources of evidence: their observations (qualitative data) of different parts of the stream table, two kinds of measurements (quantitative data) of the

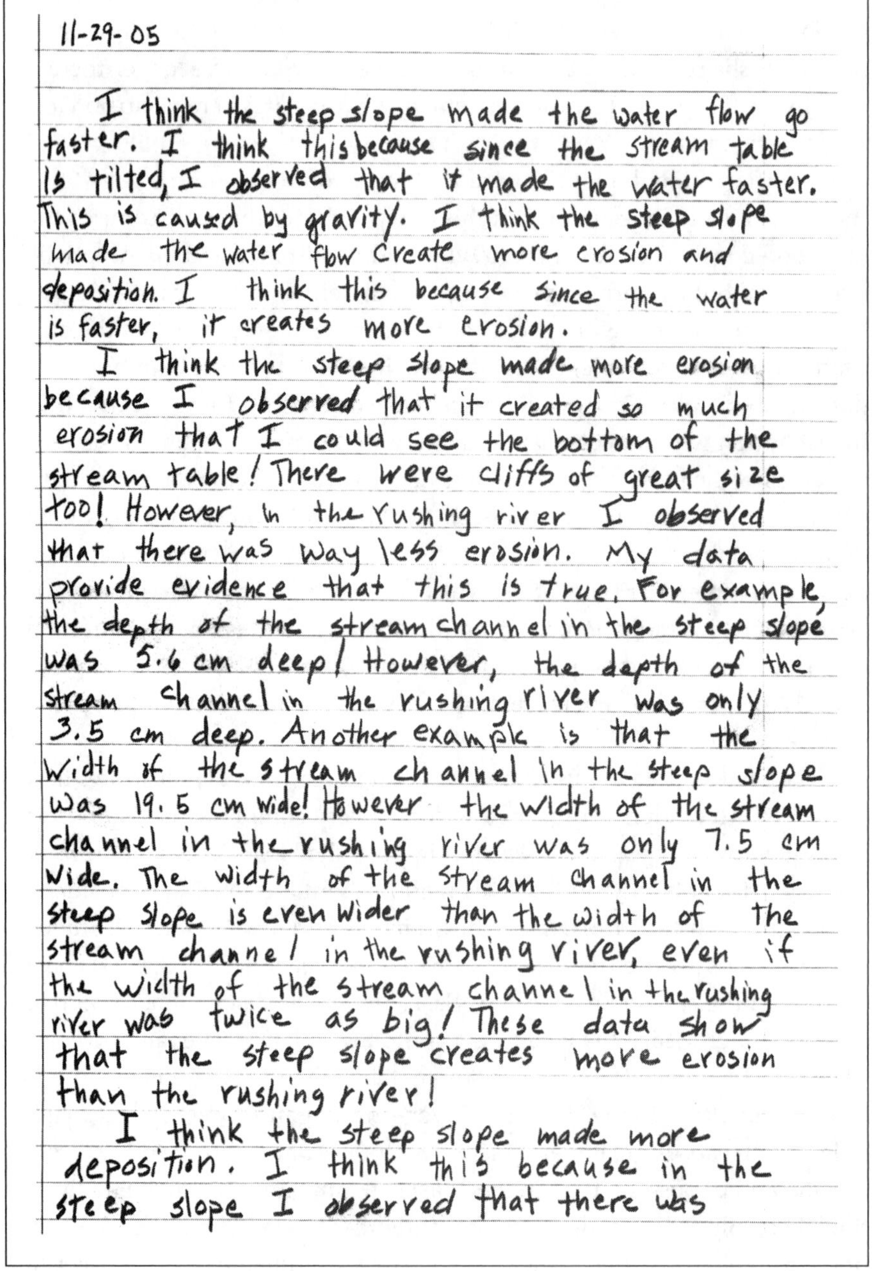

> 11-29-05
>
> I think the steep slope made the water flow go faster. I think this because since the stream table is tilted, I observed that it made the water faster. This is caused by gravity. I think the steep slope made the water flow create more erosion and deposition. I think this because since the water is faster, it creates more erosion.
>
> I think the steep slope made more erosion because I observed that it created so much erosion that I could see the bottom of the stream table! There were cliffs of great size too! However, in the rushing river I observed that there was way less erosion. My data provide evidence that this is true. For example, the depth of the stream channel in the steep slope was 5.6 cm deep! However, the depth of the stream channel in the rushing river was only 3.5 cm deep. Another example is that the width of the stream channel in the steep slope was 19.5 cm wide! However the width of the stream channel in the rushing river was only 7.5 cm wide. The width of the stream channel in the steep slope is even wider than the width of the stream channel in the rushing river, even if the width of the stream channel in the rushing river was twice as big! These data show that the steep slope creates more erosion than the rushing river!
>
> I think the steep slope made more deposition. I think this because in the steep slope I observed that there was

FIGURE 5–21 Calvin's complex conclusion

erosion in the stream channel, and three types of measurements of deposition at the end of the stream table. To prove their points, they also must compare these data with corresponding data from the "Rushing River" investigation.

During the class discussion of the "Basic Stream" investigation, Calvin's teacher lists the students' observations and data in a vertical so much deposition that it clogged up the lake that water can't even go through the hole into the dump bucket! We had to shovel away soil from the hole so water can go through! However, in the rushing river, I observed that there was not as much deposition as the steep slope. My data provide evidence that this is true. For example, the width of the deposition in the steep slope was 23.5 cm wide! However, the width of the deposition in the rushing river was only 19 cm wide. Another example is that the length of the deposition in the steep slope was 21 cm long! However, the length of the deposition in the rushing river was only 14.5 cm long. Also, the depth of the deposition in the steep slope was 4.5 cm deep! However, the depth of the deposition in the rushing river was only 1 cm deep. If the depth of the deposition in the rushing river was 4 times deeper, the steep slope will still be deeper!

Therefore, I think that a steep slope causes more deposition too. My prediction was correct because I predicted that the steep slope will create more erosion.

FIGURE 5–21 Continued

column. As the students discuss each subsequent investigation, she adds their observations and data in adjacent columns, creating a table that organizes the observations and data so that students easily can see the contrasts among them as they talk about the investigations. This is another application of the T-chart strategy (described in the "Comparisons" section of Chapter 4), which supports students in recognizing contrasting observations and data, then serves as a graphic organizer for their writing.

In this fifth-grade classroom, many students are learning English. Consequently, the teacher provides quite a detailed writing frame to guide them in writing their complex conclusions. Calvin, who writes this complex entry, speaks only Chinese at home and talks very little in class. He has qualified for the district's program for the gifted, which he will enter in sixth grade, and has strong writing skills. The following is what he chooses to use from the frame:

Water flow paragraph:	I think the steep slope made the water flow _____ . I think this because _____ .
Erosion paragraph:	I think the steep slope made _____ . However, in the _____ , I observed _____ . My data provide evidence that _____ . For example, _____ . However, _____ .
Deposition paragraph:	[Same as paragraph above]
Concluding paragraph:	Therefore, I think that a steep slope causes _____ . My prediction was _____ because I predicted _____ .

Calvin uses his observations and his data tables as he cites his evidence, which is detailed and accurate, and expresses his excitement about the greater impacts of the water on the land in the "Steep Slope" investigation. He also includes derived data he has calculated by comparing how much greater the erosion and deposition are as compared with the data in the "Rushing River" investigation.

Calvin's conclusion, of course, is a rough draft because it is a notebook entry. The next step in instruction for students with such strong skills is to help them develop more independence and fluency in their writing. Using the Useful Words and Phrases in Scientific Writing chart shown in Figure 4–26 (and Appendix A) helps them learn some other words for indicating contrasts, for example. Students also should learn to include only the most dramatic data rather than all the data (about erosion and deposition, for example, in Calvin's entry).

Calvin's conclusion shows strong scientific thinking, conceptual understanding, and scientific writing skills, especially for a bilingual child in early fifth grade. This entry, and the others in this chapter, exemplify the effect of a number of important components in science and expository writing instruction:

■ a meaningful inquiry-based science investigation
■ a thoughtful class discussion in which scientific thinking and language are modeled and practiced
■ modeling that shows students how to use tables and writing frames as organizers for their thinking and writing.

The result of such instruction is that students of varying abilities can explain and write conclusions that are organized, logical, well substantiated with evidence, and conceptually accurate. This is one of the main goals in teaching elementary students of all ages and abilities how to think and write scientifically.

CHAPTER SIX

Assessing Science Notebook Entries

A critical part of successfully integrating the teaching and learning of inquiry-based science and expository writing is determining how you will assess notebook entries in ways that will benefit both your instruction and your students' learning. As you initially plan the instruction for a science unit, you can make such decisions by considering the following questions:

■ What is the purpose of the assessment?
■ How will you assess notebook entries and provide positive, constructive feedback?
■ When and how often will you be able realistically to assess entries effectively?
■ What should you assess? What do you want students to know and be able to do?

Over the years of the Science Notebooks Program, we have developed strategies and protocols for assessing student notebook entries that teachers believe improve their instruction and help students learn. This chapter presents the rationale and components of this approach to assessing elementary science notebooks.

A Rationale for Formative, Unscored Assessment of Elementary Science Notebooks

Seattle's Science Notebooks Program has always seen science notebook assessment from a perspective that numerous studies support. First of all, the audience for the notebook writing is not the classroom teacher. The audience is other scientists. Typically, teachers' feedback to students might begin with, "I really like what you wrote here." Students are in the position of trying to please this "I" voice or locus of control. But what is truly important about the entry is what another *scientist* would notice. So a more effective response—establishing scientists as the audience—might be, "Another scientist would value this entry because you clearly have described what you have observed about that mineral and the results of your tests. For example, you included . . . . These scientific details will help the scientist understand what you are discovering about this mineral." This comment is specific to the kinds of scientific skills the student is developing and clearly indicates that the assessment criteria are those of science and scientists rather than something created and controlled by the classroom teacher.

Research supports this view. Wynne Harlen, an international leader in science-education reform, has noted that formative assessment is based on a rationale in which learning is seen "as a process of action by the learner. The focus is on learners 'doing the learning' by constructing meaning from their experiences and making sense of the world in terms of concepts and mental models. This is a constructivist view of learning which contrasts with the behaviorist view that learning is a response to external stimuli and is very much in control of the teacher" (Harlen 2004, 9).

In research about formative assessment, another point is clear: For assessment feedback to be effective, it must provide nonjudgmental re-marks without grades or rubric scores. When students receive rubric scores or rubric scores with feedback, their performance and learning do not improve and their motivation is adversely affected. However, if students are given specific constructive feedback—without scores—they have much more positive responses, including increased motivation, especially when the feedback helps them determine what they need to do next (Butler 1987, 1988).

Furthermore, when teachers use the notebooks formatively—assessing entries throughout the unit, using what they learn to improve their instruction, and providing students with constructive feedback—their students improve their performance and learning.

> Research studies have shown that, if pupils are given only marks or grades, they do not benefit from the feedback. . . . Feedback has been shown to improve learning when it gives each pupil specific guidance on strengths and weaknesses, preferably without any overall marks. Thus the way in which test results are reported to pupils so that they can identify their own strengths and weaknesses is critical. Pupils must be given the means and opportunities to work with evidence of their difficulties. For formative purposes, a test at the end of a unit or teaching module is pointless; it is too late to work with the results. We conclude that the feedback on tests, seatwork, and homework should give each pupil guidance on how to improve, and each pupil must be given help and an opportunity to work on the improvement. (Black and Wiliam 1998, 8)

The "How to Assess Science Notebook Entries" section later in this chapter explains how to give such feedback.

Another crucial finding of research on formative assessment is its effect, when done appropriately, on students who typically do not score well on any kind of test:

> Perhaps the most significant finding from the research is that the practice of formative assessment benefits all students, but the increase in levels of achievement is particularly marked for lower achieving students. Thus the effect is to decrease the gap between the more and less well achieving students. This contrasts with the evidence of the impact of [high-stakes] tests, which favour the higher achieving students and create a downward spiral for the lower achieving students, whose constant failure leads to loss of self-esteem and effort. (Harlen 2004, 9)

This research specifically reports about how high-stakes tests and scores negatively affect lower-achieving students. But even without giving students scored feedback, teachers can negatively impact students' self-esteem. So teachers must be aware of what kind of constructive feedback they provide. All students, but particularly lower-achieving students, need to receive feedback that specifically identifies their strengths and addresses their weaknesses in ways that increase their self-esteem while engaging them in improving their entry. (Some strategies for providing such feedback are included later in this chapter.)

Programs and teachers make a legitimate argument about the need for scored assessments in school systems in which grades and scores are the primary, required means of accountability. In the Science Notebooks Program, we have addressed this challenge by using the science notebooks solely for formative purposes. Teachers do not score any entries but provide constructive feedback throughout the unit.

To solve the problem of grading, teachers can start the unit by giving students an assessment, which teachers score and keep in their student files. At the end of the unit, students take a summative assessment, which the teacher compares with the earlier unit assessment and scores. If a student's work in the science notebook indicates that the student has stronger skills and deeper conceptual understanding than the scored summative assessment indicates, then the teacher might photocopy pages of the notebook to serve as anecdotal evidence of the student's skills and knowledge.

In this approach, teachers never score the science notebook entries but still have summative scores to use in reporting student achievement. This solves what Harlen identifies as a challenge in summative assessments, including high-stakes assessments administered by districts or states: "The challenge is to conduct summative assessment in such a way that does not have a negative impact on students' motivation for learning" (Harlen 2004, 9). The vast majority of the students' assessment experiences in science in this integrated science-writing approach are formative, positive, constructive, and free of scoring. As a result, students' self-esteem and motivation are much more affected by ongoing constructive, unscored feedback of the work they do in their science notebooks than by a single score they receive for a summative test that they do outside their work in the notebook.

When to Assess Science Notebook Entries

Over the years of the Science Notebooks Program, we have found that teachers can provide the most effective constructive feedback if they assess the notebooks three or four times, depending on the science unit. During each lesson, you should check that all students are writing in their notebooks. But you do not need to scrutinize and respond to every entry in order to be effective in your assessment. In fact, when teachers make comments about every entry, they do not have time to provide constructive remarks and, instead, resort to such unproductive feedback as "Nice job" and "Good thinking," or perhaps smiley faces or stickers.

Instead, assess notebooks after a series of three or four lessons that have been developing students' understanding of certain concepts and/or building specific scientific skills (such as making and writing observations). For example, in the *Sound* unit, published by Science and Technology for Children (STC), third graders conduct a series of investigations in which they discover that the length of an object affects the pitch it makes. They build their understanding of this concept through experiences with tuning forks, nails, and then rulers. After students finish their entries about their investigation of the rulers, teachers collect the students' science notebooks. With each notebook, they skim through the first entries to get a general idea of what the student has written (as teachers have been doing throughout each lesson as students are writing). Then they carefully read the last entry about rulers and provide detailed constructive feedback.

If you read entries in this way three to five times during a unit that lasts about six to twelve weeks (depending on how often you teach science per week), you will have time to give valuable feedback that can help students develop deeper understanding and stronger skills. You also will be better able to determine what you need to change or keep the same as you plan further instruction.

What to Assess in Science Notebook Entries

Chapters 1 and 2 explain what the Science Notebooks Program expects students to include in science notebook entries and why. But essentially, we expect students to write in their notebooks during and/or after every science lesson, write a date for each entry, and include a focus or investigative question for each lesson. The content of each entry varies depending on what *thinking* and *science concepts* are most critical in the lesson, what type of *expository writing experience* is most suited to developing students' conceptual understanding, and the *critical thinking* and *writing skills* for that lesson.

This approach focuses the students' writing energy on these aspects of science because elementary students have limited time and energy for their science writing—we want to maximize their learning by focusing the writing. In other approaches, students might be expected to write their procedures so that fellow students or scientists can replicate their experiment. Yet another, more self-reflective and metacognitive approach has students write about what they have learned, how they have learned, what they think their ideas mean in a context beyond their investigation, and what further questions they would like to explore in other experiments. These are valuable aspects of scientists' work. We have chosen to have students *talk* about these aspects but focus their writing in a disciplined and structured way.

To determine what to assess in science notebooks, consider what you expect students to know and be able to do by the end of the unit as well as at the end of each lesson or groups of lessons. As explained in Chapter 1, teachers using this integrated science-writing approach expect students to:

- Develop *conceptual understanding* of the *science content, or "big ideas,"* of the unit.
- *Think scientifically*, applying critical thinking skills in solving problems and developing conceptual understanding.
- Use *scientific skills* effectively.
- Communicate scientific thinking and science concepts through *expository writing*.

Expository Writing Skills

To be effective, your assessment must focus on what is most important in a particular notebook entry in terms of what it reveals about the students' scientific thinking, skills, and/or understanding in that lesson or investigation. Therefore, when you look at student entries, which are always rough drafts in a science notebook, do not assess conventions (grammar, punctuation, and spelling), handwriting, and neatness. Instead, focus on the following traits of the writing:

- *Content.* Are students writing clearly and accurately about the concepts they have learned through a scientific inquiry or investigation? Are they communicating effectively, in a focused way, about their scientific thinking, including providing appropriate evidence to support their claims?
- *Organization.* Are students organizing their entries in appropriate ways depending on what they are communicating? Comparisons and conclusions, for example, have different structures because the process of logically thinking through them is distinctive for each form (as explained in Chapters 4 and 5). Do students use appropriate transition words (for example, *first, next, then, finally*) to organize and present their thinking?

- *Word choice*. Do students use scientific terms accurately? Do they use general scientific language (for example, "The data provide evidence") to structure their scientific writing?

These writing traits are integrally connected with conceptual understanding, scientific skills, and scientific thinking.

Generally, you do not need to address any *weakness* in an entry in terms of *sentence fluency* (the variety of sentence structure and flow of the sentences). The exception is when students show particular *strengths* in this trait that contribute to the effectiveness of their entries. Similarly, do not assess the trait of *voice* (when students reveal a strong sense of themselves as individual scientists). As with sentence fluency, call attention to voice only if students are clearly demonstrating this trait in ways that contribute to the scientific strengths of their entries.

Criteria for Exemplary Entries

The Criteria for Exemplary Science Notebook Entries chart (Figure 6–1) shows generic criteria for assessing the four components of notebook entries: science concepts or "big ideas," scientific skills, critical thinking, and expository writing. To stay focused as you assess notebooks—either by yourself or with a group of teachers—you can use these guidelines. For each entry, you will need to be clear about the *specific* concepts, skills, thinking, and expository writing that students are expected to know or be able to do at the end of the lesson or series of lessons. (The "How to Assess Science Notebook Entries" section later in this chapter explains the actual assessment process.)

Examples of Formative Assessment

Symphony, a first grader, wrote the notebook entries shown in Figures 6–2 and 6–3. (All the entries from her notebook are shown in Appendix B.) Her class has been studying *Balls and Ramps*, a unit published by Insights. Symphony and her classmates attend a Seattle public school in which 75 percent of the students receive free or reduced-price lunch. Over 50 percent of the students are African American, about 25 percent are Asian, about 20 percent are Latino, and about 5 percent are Caucasian.

When students were writing independently in their notebooks during this unit, their teacher circulated throughout the classroom, checking that all students were writing, and assisting students who needed extra support (as explained in Chapter 2).

Although this is a primary classroom, the assessment process is the same as for intermediate elementary students: After a series of lessons in the unit, collect the notebooks and assess an entry thoroughly, using the process described in the previous section. After several more lessons, do this again. Then repeat the process after several more lessons.

Criteria for Exemplary Science Notebook Entries

Conceptual Understanding	Scientific Skills and Thinking	Expository Writing
Understanding of "big ideas" of unit Demonstrates, through words and graphics, an accurate and quite full grasp of the major science concepts that were introduced ** May demonstrate one or more of the following: ■ Appropriately/accurately applies previous learning to new concepts and skills ■ Extends the new concept or skill to new problems or new phenomena	*Use of scientific inquiry skills* Thorough and purposeful use of skills to advance learning. For example: ■ Makes accurate and full observations, with complete records ■ Collects and records data accurately, completely, and honestly ■ Examines data and identifies results (for example, by comparing different data points) ■ Shows understanding of fair tests or controlled investigations *Use of evidence to support explanations* Demonstrates understanding of relationship between data and explanation: ■ Supports explanations with appropriate data *Use of critical thinking skills to draw inferences* Demonstrates understanding of relationships between data and inference: ■ Draws reasonable inferences from data; supports inferences with reasoning	*Idea/content (development)* Has control of content: ■ States information or idea clearly ■ Develops information or idea fully with relevant details, evidence, and explanation *Organization (sequence)* ■ Uses different text structures to organize ideas/information effectively ■ Logically sequences or groups details ■ Uses appropriate transition words to show logical connections *Word choice* ■ Uses scientific vocabulary accurately ■ Uses nonscientific vocabulary effectively to clarify and explain *** These traits *may* be apparent: *Voice (authority)* ■ Has an engaged voice that shows confidence with scientific stance ■ May include self-reflection *Sentence fluency (sentence structure and variety)* ■ Can use multiple types of clauses and structures to clarify and develop ideas

Adaptation of chart by Inverness Research Associates, July 2002.

FIGURE 6–1 Criteria for exemplary notebook entries

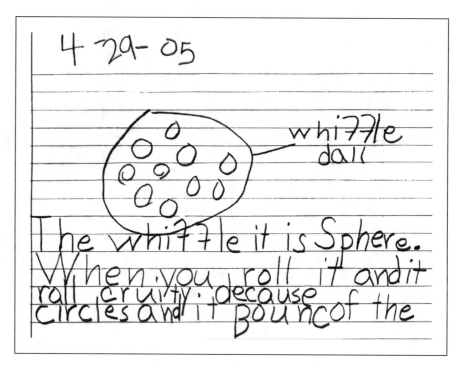

FIGURE 6–2 Symphony's entry after four lessons

Symphony wrote the entry shown in Figure 6–2 after four lessons in which the class had been investigating and discussing the properties of balls and how different properties affect how the balls move—specifically, how they bounce and roll. Her teacher has recorded the students' observations on a class table that includes columns for the properties of color, shape, size, weight, texture, and "other," which includes miscellaneous observations about the sounds the balls make when they hit the hard ground, and their structure (hollow or solid). Students refer to this table of properties as they are writing so that they think about which properties they need to address in their entry.

The students have been observing and discussing a number of different balls. This lesson is an embedded assessment—students observe a whiffle ball, which they have not yet investigated. Then they write about it just as they have in previous lessons except that in this case, the teacher does not model how to write the entry so that he will be able to assess how well the students think and write independently.

In assessing this entry thoroughly, first consider the "big ideas" or science concepts that students would need to know at this point in the unit:

■ Balls have properties.
■ These properties can affect how balls move.
■ Specific properties make balls move in particular ways.

The main scientific skills they would need to have developed would be the ability to:

- make accurate and full observations
- compare test outcomes from different balls
- draw reasonable inferences from observations; support inferences with evidence.

Scientific thinking skills would include the ability to:

- draw reasonable inferences based on observations and tests of *unfamiliar* balls.

In their expository writing, students would be expected to mention three to four properties of the whiffle ball, and state how they think or infer the properties might affect how the ball moves. This reflects the idea/content and organization traits. Students also would use words such as *whiffle ball, sphere, bounce, roll, hollow,* and *light* in describing the ball's properties.

In this entry, Symphony has written the date in numerals, as required. She does not write a question because that was not needed in this case. In her illustration, she draws circles to represent holes, which she also mentions in her written description. She also draws an appropriate number of circles. This is evidence of the strength in the idea/content trait through an illustration. She gives the illustration a title, which is a requirement in making scientific illustrations because other people need to understand clearly what she is communicating in her drawing.

Symphony writes: "The whiffle it is Sphere. When you roll it and it roll cruity [crookity/crookedly] decause [because] of the circles and it Bounc[.]" This written part of the entry is strong in that she mentions the ball's shape using appropriate word choice (*sphere*). She also identifies its dominant observable property—its circles, or holes. She names two ways in which the ball moves—it rolls and it bounces. And she describes the way in which it rolls—"cruity"—and why she infers that it behaves that way—"decause of the circles."

The entry shows then that she understands that balls have properties, some of which affect how they move. To determine this about an unfamiliar kind of ball, she has to have made accurate observations. She states an observation about how the ball rolls, then provides a reasonable inference about the property that has caused that behavior, which reflects strong scientific thinking. She also has used scientific vocabulary, including the word *because.*

The weaknesses of the entry are that she has included only two properties (its shape and its holes or texture). She also does not describe how it bounced. But she does not seem to have any misconceptions. (Using the word *circles* instead of *holes* is most likely an issue of language usage rather than conceptual confusion.) In reflecting about further instruction for Symphony, we would want to help her develop the habit of reading each entry after she finishes it. This will develop her ability to revise her own work independently, an essential writing skill. With practice, she also will include more in her writing.

In responding to this particular entry during a conference with her, you would talk about the points mentioned above. If you write the comments and questions on a sticky note, you will have to be much briefer. To a first grader, depending on her reading skills, you might write something like the following:

> Your illustration shows details about one property—the holes. You also *write* about two properties, two ways the ball moved, and why you think it rolls crookedly. Another scientist would really understand some important information about what you have learned so far about this ball! What else would he or she want to know about how it bounces? Why do you think it bounces like it does? Did you notice anything about its weight or what is inside it?

Weeks later, the class conducts an investigation in the unit's twelfth lesson. Its main *concept* or "big idea" is:

- Balls of different mass (referred to as *weight* in first grade) roll down a ramp at the same speed when all other variables are controlled or kept the same.

In terms of *scientific skills*, students need to know how to:

- Conduct a fair test (a controlled investigation). In this case, students determine that they must use identical ramps, set them up at the same angle, release balls at the same place and in the same way, and so on.
- Discuss and make sense of the data.
- Summarize the results, then use those data as evidence for their explanation of what they learned through their investigation.

Their *scientific thinking* is reflected in the way they present their reasoning in their conclusion. In terms of *expository writing*, students need to be able to:

- Write a conclusion that reports the outcomes of the investigation, including appropriate data, and answers the investigative question. (Chapter 5 explains how to teach students about the components of a strong scientific conclusion.)

Symphony wrote the entry in Figure 6–3 at the end this twelfth lesson, about five weeks after the previous entry. She begins with the date and the investigative question, circling the words she thinks are important. (Each student does this, then the whole class discusses the question.) She then makes a T-chart and records the results of her group's tests by appropriately using tally marks. (Each student records test results so that everyone has the experience and so that more than one person is recording the data.) A "tie" means there was no real difference between when the two balls reached the bottom of their respective ramps. "No tie" means that there was a significant difference.

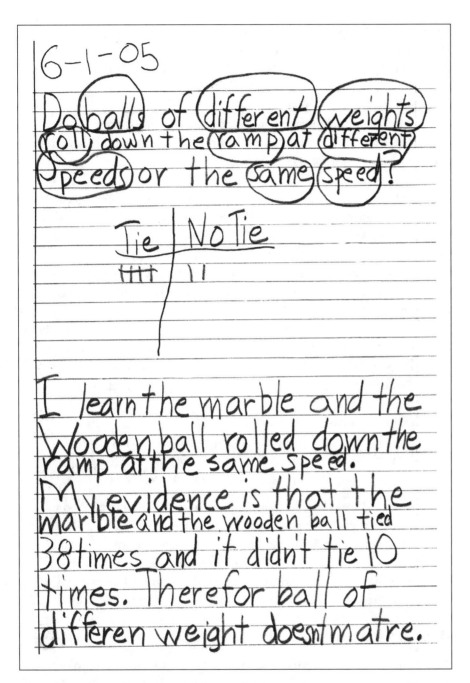

FIGURE 6–3 Symphony's entry after twelve lessons

Symphony begins her conclusion by reporting the qualitative (comparative) results of the investigation that answer the question: "I learn the marble and the Wooden ball rolled down the ramp at the same speed." In this statement, she identifies the two balls, uses words from the question, and accurately reports the overall results.

Then she provides quantitative (measured) data from the class data table. (Each group contributes its test results to a group data table, and students then discuss that cumulative data and write about it in their own conclusions. This is why this student does not use the data from her T-chart.) She uses the phrase "My evidence is" to introduce the data that support her conclusion: "My evidence is that the marble and the wooden ball tied 38 times and it didn't tie 10 times."

Finally, she uses *therefore* to introduce her concluding statement: "Therefor ball of differen weight doesnt matre." The concluding statement is reasonable given the data she provides.

In terms of conceptual understanding, the entry is accurate: balls of different mass (weight) do roll down a ramp at the same speed in a controlled investigation. We cannot assess here how she conducted her investigation, but we know that she made a data table (the T-chart) and recorded test results. In her writing, she clearly knows the components of a conclusion in that she answers the question in a general way, provides data as evidence, then makes a concluding statement that is supported by both the qualitative and quantitative data she provides.

This conclusion also indicates that Symphony can think critically about the test results and interpret what they mean in terms of a science concept: "weight doesnt matre." Finally, she is able to use text structures—words from the question, "My evidence is" for providing data, and "Therefore" to introduce a concluding statement—to organize and communicate her data and thinking in an articulate way.

Symphony, then, has written a strong entry. The only weakness is that she did not reread her writing, which was a problem with her earlier entry as well. In providing feedback on a sticky note, her teacher might write:

> This is a strong entry because you wrote about what happened in the tests. Then you gave your evidence. Finally, you used "therefore" and wrote about the big idea about weight. This is important information and scientific thinking! When scientists finish writing, they always read what they have written. Why don't you reread your entry, too, to be sure that it will make sense to other scientists?

Overall Assessment

Assessing elementary students' science notebooks is not going to provide a complete picture of what students know about the unit's science concepts and what they are able to do in terms of scientific skills and thinking. Elementary students, particularly in the primary grades, are not sophisticated enough in their writing skills to communicate at the highest levels of their knowledge and reasoning. Moreover, to assess many of the scientific skills, teachers need to observe students actively engaged in scientific investigations—setting up tests, using tools, solving problems, interacting with classmates, and so on.

To assess these skills, you will need to observe and talk with your students and make mental notes as well as either writing notes on checklists (provided in teacher's guides) or on sticky notes, which you place in a file for each student. This observation process will help you plan and adjust instruction as needed to meet their needs. It also will give you written, anecdotal evidence of your students' strengths and weaknesses.

The file for each student also will include your assessment sheet notes (see the next section) about the strengths and weaknesses in an entry, and further instruction plans. By the end of a science unit, you will have enough anecdotal records—in addition to a scored summative assessment—to give you a good idea of what each student knows and is able to do. You then can use this information in narrative reports about your students' academic progress in science and expository writing.

How to Assess Science Notebook Entries

Before you assess a notebook entry from a science lesson, think about the goals of the lesson: What concepts, scientific skills and thinking, and expository writing do you expect the students to have learned and how do you expect to see this learning reflected in the entry? Figure 6–4 provides a structure that can guide your thinking. Begin by looking quickly through the entries that precede the entry you want to assess. This will give you a sense of what the student has been writing in the notebook. (If you spot-checked students' notebooks as you walked around the classroom while students were writing independently, you probably will not discover major lapses in the entries now.) You do not need to make any comments about these entries unless, when you are writing feedback about the one entry, you need to refer the student to earlier entries that may support or conflict with the entry you are assessing.

Next, think about the lesson for the entry you are assessing:

- What is (are) the science concept(s) or "big idea(s)" of the lesson or investigation, and how does (do) it (they) relate to the development of the science content or concepts throughout the unit?
- What scientific skills and thinking are important in this lesson or investigation?
- What structures and language are important in the expository writing?
- What is (are) the lesson's focus or investigative question(s) to which the student is responding in this entry? (This question is not always the same one students will write below the date at the beginning of an entry. See Chapter 7 for information about these questions.)

To guide your assessment of the four components in the entry—"big ideas" or conceptual understanding, scientific skills, scientific or critical thinking, and expository writing—use the Criteria for Exemplary Science Notebook Entries chart (Figure 6–1). With these in mind, skim the entry, then reread it carefully, considering each of these criteria. Start with the *strengths* of each component in the entry *without thinking about the weaknesses*. (If you are assessing science notebooks with a group of teachers, do not even mention a weakness at this point.) Note the strengths on the Assessing Student Work form (Figure 6–4).

Interestingly, in their feedback of the Science Notebooks Program, the vast majority of teachers write about how difficult it is for them to focus first on students' strengths. Because teachers are charged with improving student achievement, they fall into a counterproductive pattern of focusing on weaknesses in students' performance. This is especially detrimental for low-achieving students, who rarely have any awareness of their strengths.

One of the most effective ways of learning how to see past an entry's weaknesses is to look at student work with other teachers at the same grade level. Teachers who participate in science-writing reflection groups in our program report that they spent little time focusing on their students' strengths until other teachers assessed their students' notebook entries. They also report, in overwhelming numbers, how powerful it is to notice strengths that they totally had overlooked until other teachers identified them. (See the "Science-Writing Reflection Groups" section that follows.)

Providing Constructive Feedback

In providing constructive feedback to students about their science notebook entries, consider the following:

1. Address the strengths first, and point out specific examples of what you are talking about. It is not enough to say, "You've written a strong scientific entry." You need to identify the specific strengths on the page.

2. Never use the word *but* in constructive feedback. This negates any positive remarks you have made prior to using this word (for example, "This was a strong entry because you did [such and such]. *But . . . ."*). Few students—especially low-achieving students—will remember anything except what you said after *but*, and they may not remember those words either because of the negativity.

3. Address the weaknesses by asking questions such as, "What do you think another scientist might be interested in knowing, or need to know, about . . . ?" "Did you find out anything else that might help another scientist understand the results of your tests?"

4. With struggling students who have low skills and self-esteem, address only the strengths. Help them understand specifically what they have done well in terms of the science-assessment criteria. Then, after they have developed more self-confidence and skills, ask them questions so that, in answering the queries, the students improve their entries.

The most effective means of communicating such feedback is a conference. When this is not practical, write comments on a sticky note, then put it on the entry. (Refer to earlier examples of feedback for Figures 6–2 and 6–3.) Schedule time for students to look at your feedback, reread their entries, and respond to your feedback by talking with you and revising their entries

Assessing Student Work and Planning Instruction

1. Look briefly at each entry prior to the one you are assessing to give you a general idea of the quality of the student's entries.
2. Before assessing the selected entry, think about the:
   - science concept(s)/ "big idea(s)" of the lesson/investigation and how it (they) related to the development of concepts in the unit;
   - scientific skills and thinking that may be involved in the lesson/investigation;
   - important structures and language in the expository writing;
   - question(s) to which the student may be responding in the entry.
3. Follow the Criteria for Exemplary Science Notebook Entries chart (Figure 6–1) as you assess the entry.
   - Skim the entry. Then reread it carefully, considering each of these criteria. (Do *not* consider other criteria.)
   - *Note strengths of each component first*, then weaknesses. Determine further instruction for student or class.
   - Write constructive feedback on a sticky note and place it on the entry.

Strengths	Weaknesses	Further Instruction

FIGURE 6–4 Guidelines for assessment and planning

when necessary. (It is appropriate for students to revise their entries except that they should not change their predictions or data so that they can have "the right answers.") With young students and students with undeveloped reading skills, read the note together and discuss their responses to and questions about your feedback.

To respect the integrity of your students' scientific work, *do not write directly in the students' notebooks*. These entries are rough drafts, but they also are permanent records of your students' scientific investigations and thinking. Teacher comments should not be an indelible part of their work.

Science-Writing Reflection Groups

To enhance your assessment and to experience the professional benefits of working in a collaborative situation, you also might want to assess notebook entries with other teachers. In the Science Notebooks Program, about sixty teachers meet monthly in grade-level teams to plan the science-writing instruction for their science units and critique student notebook entries. They teach three units each year, so for each unit, they meet one month to plan instruction, the next month to critique student entries from a selected lesson, and the third month to look at complete notebooks. A teacher in each group facilitates the work following protocols that we have developed in the program. You can use this same process in working with your grade-level colleagues at your school.

Instructional Planning Meetings

Planning and adjusting instruction to meet students' needs is an important part of formative assessment. In the planning meeting, discuss the lessons in your unit, concentrating on those that will be most challenging. The protocol in Figure 6–5 will keep the group focused on the four components that you will consider in your assessment—science content or "big ideas" in the unit and each lesson, scientific skills, scientific thinking, and expository writing. The emphasis is on instruction and what you all need to anticipate in your planning. The group facilitator should keep the group centered on the planning sheet so that you all stay on task and do not discuss other criteria and issues (for example, handwriting or spelling, your students' or school issues) that can undermine the group's productivity. You can take notes on the sheet to help you later as you plan your actual lessons.

Meetings for Assessing Single Notebook Entries

The protocol for assessing single entries with a group of teachers (see Figure 6–6) follows virtually the same process as the one you use in assessing your own students' entries. However, because teachers are looking at entries from other teachers' students, the facilitator needs to ensure that the teacher whose student's work is being critiqued does *not* explain anything about the student or the entry. We have found this to be extremely effective

Science-Writing Reflection Groups
Protocol for Instructional Planning Meetings

The facilitator's role is to ensure that the protocol is followed.

For each lesson you are planning:

1. Reflect about the *"big ideas"/concepts* of the lesson and how they relate to the development of concepts throughout the unit.
2. Consider the *scientific skills and thinking* that may be involved in the investigation.
3. Think about the *expository writing skills* students will need in order to communicate their understanding and thinking in the lesson.
4. Consider the lesson's *focus/investigative question(s) and/or the reflective question(s)* to which the students may be responding in the entry.
5. Discuss the *challenges* students could face in terms of points 1 through 4.
6. Determine *what the teacher will need to model* before the lesson and/or the writing.

At the end of the meeting, plan what student work each teacher will bring to the next meeting.

Unit Title _____ *Date* _____

Lesson	Notes

FIGURE 6–5 Protocol for planning meetings

Science-Writing Reflection Groups
Protocol for Assessing Notebook Entries

The facilitator's role is to ensure that the protocol is followed.

1. Consider the specific concepts, scientific skills and thinking, and expository writing that pertain to the selected lesson and entry.
2. Briefly go over the Criteria for Exemplary Science Notebook Entries chart (Figure 6–1), which presents the general standards we expect students to meet in the notebook entries. Discuss the criteria in terms of the entry you will be assessing.
3. Silently, and fairly quickly, read through the first student sample without looking for anything in particular.

   ■ The teacher who provides the sample should *not* explain anything about the student or the entry.

4. Read the entry again, focusing on only the strengths in terms of the criteria.
5. Discuss the *strengths* of the sample:

   ■ Do *not* mention any weaknesses.
   ■ Do *not* discuss any other criteria (e.g., neatness, conventions— spelling, punctuation, grammar).
   ■ List the strengths on the Assessing Student Work and Planning Instruction form (Figure 6–4). All teachers can do this, or one teacher can volunteer to record these notes for the teacher whose student's entry is being assessed.

6. Discuss the *weaknesses* of the sample in terms of the criteria.

   ■ List the weaknesses on the assessment form.

7. Discuss and plan further instruction and feedback that could build on the strengths and improve the weaknesses.

   ■ Make notes on the form regarding further instruction.

8. Give a completed form to the teacher whose student's entry was assessed.

FIGURE 6–6 Protocol for assessing single entries

(although frustrating for some teachers) because the other teachers then see the entry totally from their own perspectives. This enables them to notice things about the work that the student's teacher may not have noticed. (This is especially important in assessing the work of low-achieving students.) In fact, teachers frequently are amazed by what they see in their students' work during these sessions. Focusing on the strengths first also allows *all* the teachers to notice aspects of the work that they might have missed had they followed their natural inclination to identify weaknesses.

During the discussion of the entry, one teacher volunteers to take notes on the form shown in Figure 6–4 so that the teacher whose student's work is being critiqued can concentrate on the discussion. These notes will be useful in writing constructive feedback to the student and in planning further instruction for the student and the class.

You may find the Notes About Lessons Learned form shown in Appendix A useful for taking notes about your group's discussions of the lessons. Because you already will have taught the lessons at this point, you may need a place to write ideas about what to do when you teach the unit the next time. Then you can put the sheet in your lesson files for future reference. Our teachers feel that this practice has helped them increase their efficiency and effectiveness in teaching the units from year to year.

Meetings for Assessing Whole Notebooks

These meetings work in the same way as the first two. The main difference is that you cannot assess every entry in each notebook during these sessions. So you first must skim quickly through an entire notebook, using small sticky notes to mark entries that you would like to come back to and discuss with the whole group.

In assessing a completed science notebook with other teachers, you are looking for cumulative evidence of the degree to which the student has developed conceptual understanding, scientific skills and thinking, and expository writing skills that are important in that particular science unit. The purpose of this group work is not necessarily to arrive at a summative judgment about the quality of the child's work, but rather to go through a collaborative process of assessment in which the teachers in the group reach deeper levels of understanding about what to look for in student work and how to solve challenges in science instruction.

Classroom teachers on their own generally do not have time to analyze whole notebooks in this way at the completion of a unit. Nor do you need to if, after every three to five lessons, you go through the process of carefully assessing a single entry for every student and providing constructive feedback, as described earlier. However, using this approach in assessing science notebooks with other teachers is a powerful way to deepen your appreciation and understanding of what the science notebooks can reveal about student skills and understanding as well as effective instructional practices in science.

Effects of This Assessment Approach

The end result of implementing this approach in assessing elementary science notebooks—in a group or by yourself—is that you are aware throughout the unit of how students are progressing in developing their science knowledge and skills. As a result, you can adjust your instruction as necessary and much more effectively meet the needs of the students as they experience different lessons.

You also provide meaningful feedback three or four times during a unit. This feedback is positive and constructive, and engages students in improving their entries, not because they have not received the highest score, but because they are addressing questions that other scientists might have about their notebook entries. Thus students are able to focus on their work as scientists, which also increases their motivation and self-esteem, especially if they typically are low-achieving students.

References

Black, Paul, and Dylan Wiliam. 1998. "Inside the Black Box: Raising Standards Through Classroom Assessment." *Kappan Home.* www.pdkintl.org/kappan/kbla/9810.htm.

Butler, Ruth. 1987. "Task-Involving and Ego-Involving Properties of Evaluation: Effects of Different Feedback Conditions on Motivational Perceptions, Interest and Performance." *Journal of Educational Psychology* 79 (4): 474–82.

———. 1988. "Enhancing and Undermining Intrinsic Motivation: The Effects of Task-Involving and Ego-Involving Evaluation on Interest and Performance." *British Journal of Educational Psychology* 58: 1–14.

Harlen, Wynne. 2004. "The Role of Assessment in the Implementation of Science in the Primary School." Posted at www.science.uva.nl/scienceisprimary/. Plenary #2.

Stokes, Laura, Mark St. John, and Jo Fyfe. 2002. "Writing for Science, Science for Writing: A Study of the Seattle Elementary Science Expository Writing and Science Notebooks Progam." Posted at www.inverness-research.org/reports.html. Inverness, CA: Inverness Research Associates.

CHAPTER SEVEN

Planning Expository Writing Instruction for a Science Unit

The four fundamental components of the instruction, learning, and assessment in a science unit are science concepts or "big ideas," scientific skills, scientific thinking, and expository writing. Teacher's guides usually quite clearly present the first three. But the guides will not help you plan meaningful instruction and learning of the fourth component, expository writing, including more complex forms of science writing. To develop the writing component of a science unit, you will need to create your own instruction plans and materials. This chapter will help you do that.

In Seattle's Science Notebooks Program, we have developed a supplementary writing curriculum for each of our eighteen inquiry-based units. Each curriculum explains, lesson by lesson, what teachers can do so that students learn science-writing skills while also deepening their conceptual understanding and scientific skills and thinking. In developing these curricula, we go through a general process that you can use in developing your own writing lessons and materials for a science unit. The basic steps are:

1. Read the *overview* of the concepts, scientific skills, and critical thinking presented at the beginning of the teacher's guide.
2. Refer to a copy of this list as you go through the unit to see how each *concept* is developed through specific experiences, and note the *scientific skills and critical thinking* students need to learn in order to build their understanding of the science concepts.

Next, go through *each lesson* and do the following:

3. Write a *focus or investigative question* to focus the students' minds on what they will be investigating in the lesson (as explained in this chapter).
4. Determine which *graphic organizers*—for example, tables, T-charts, and system-parts maps—will help students organize their observations, data, and/or thinking (as explained in Chapters 3, 4, and 5).
5. Decide *what students need to write about* and which *expository writing skills* they should learn so that the writing experience helps them

further develop their scientific thinking and understanding (as explained in Chapters 4 and 5).

6. Determine the important *vocabulary* students need to learn after they have had concrete experiences during their investigations. Then make word cards to place in the science word bank so that students can use the words in their discussions and writing (as explained in Chapter 3).

7. Plan the *shared-writing minilesson* (explained in Chapter 2), including the thinking and skills you need to model and the writing frames and other scaffolding students can use as they independently write entries in their notebooks.

By beginning your planning with an overview of what students will learn in a unit, then looking through each lesson to see how the concepts and skills are developed, you will have a good sense of the unit's "story." Often, the lessons are designed so that students construct understanding of a particular concept through experiences in several consecutive lessons. And to develop this understanding through the lessons, students learn to use the particular scientific skills and critical thinking that help them learn the concepts.

This flow of the teaching and learning of concepts, skills, and thinking does not follow the same pattern in every unit. But the lessons do tend to fall into three broad categories, which can help you plan instruction. These are lessons in which students:

1. access prior knowledge, and/or make initial observations and comparisons

2. conduct more focused or ongoing observations and/or controlled investigations, then develop explanations or conclusions

3. apply their conceptual understanding, scientific skills, and critical thinking in finding solutions to problems and in making connections with their daily lives and the real world.

As you plan instruction for a specific lesson, determine which of these general categories describes what students are doing in the lesson. Then begin your planning by developing the focus or investigative question (as explained in the next section) because that process also will help you understand what writing experience will deepen the students' learning of the concepts and skills in that lesson.

Focus or Investigative Questions

Our teachers were thrilled when we began developing focus or investigative questions for our science units. They believe that the questions have helped significantly in improving their instruction and their students' learning. Teachers introduce this question toward the beginning of a lesson—during the engagement stage of the teaching-learning sequence (as explained in Chapter 2). The question engages, then focuses, students' minds on what they will be investigating, and helps foster the idea that science is about exploring questions. Students also often write about the question at the end of a lesson.

The focus or investigative question frames the science lesson and so must be an important question for students to contemplate as they explore with concrete materials, conduct controlled investigations, or develop their understanding and connect it to the real world. Although these questions may be implicit in published science units, they are not provided explicitly, so you will need to develop them yourself, as we did. In the more general lessons, these questions are called *focus* questions. In lessons in which students conduct controlled investigations, the questions are called *investigative* questions. Sample question stems are included in the next three sections about planning your science and writing instruction for each lesson. Figure 7–1 shows questions for *Plant Growth and Development*, a unit for third graders published by Science and Technology for Children (STC).

Planning Science-Writing Instruction for Different Types of Lessons

Each kind of lesson requires certain types of questions, organizers, and writing forms and frames to support students in developing their skills and understanding. These organizers and writing forms and frames have been explained in Chapters 3 through 6. But this integrated science-writing approach is complex, so you need succinct, graphic reminders of what to consider as you are planning. The appropriate planning chart for each lesson category is included in the next three sections.

Lessons That Focus on Prior Knowledge, Initial or General Observations, and Comparisons

These lessons are usually the first lessons in a unit and tend to be more general because students need to begin a unit of study by thinking about their prior knowledge and engaging in initial observations. They also need to develop the skill of making scientific observations. Figure 7–2 shows examples of typical focus questions, organizers, and writing frames that you can use in these types of lessons.

Before you begin these lessons, remember to establish the routine for using science notebooks. Model how to write the date in numerals at the top of the page before the lesson begins, then model how to write the focus question (or glue it in, if the students are young) during the engagement part of the lesson.

A typical stem for a focus question for a first lesson is "What do you think you know about _____ ?" The question includes the words "*think you know*" so that students make a distinction between ideas they think make sense because of prior experiences they have had, and concepts they

---

> **Focus or Investigative Questions for STC's**
> ***Plant Growth and Development* Unit for Third Grade**
>
> What can you observe about a dry bean seed?
>
> How has the bean seed changed since it has been soaking?
>
> What might happen to the seeds during the next twenty-four hours?
>
> What differences can you observe in the seedlings?
>
> What do you observe about the plant over time? What do you predict the line of the graph will look like? How tall do you predict the plant will be in the end?
>
> What did you observe during the plant's growth spurt?
>
> What do the different parts of the bee do?
>
> What do you think the different parts of the flower do for the plant?
>
> How do bees and plants help each other?
>
> How are the flowers of the plants changing?
>
> How is a model useful in learning about plants and animals?
>
> What does a model help us to know about plants and bees?
>
> How can we use a model to represent what we have learned about plants and bees?
>
> What story does the graph tell about your plant?
>
> What could you do to the plants to make them produce even more seeds?

FIGURE 7–1 Focus or investigative questions for plant unit

confirm or know through observations and investigations in science. After you introduce this question at the beginning of a lesson, students can jot down their ideas in their notebooks under the date and the question. By writing their ideas before the class discusses the question, they engage their minds with their own past experiences that relate to the subject of the question. After a class discussion, they can add more ideas to their notes. In an initial lesson like this, you do not need to plan any modeling of the writing. This kind of entry serves as a preassessment of the students' conceptual understanding.

Another common question in the first several lessons is "What can you observe about _____?" In this kind of lesson or investigation, students observe organisms, objects, or events. They also begin to develop the skill of observing scientifically, so you first must model how to use the Observations organizer (see Chapters 3 and 4). Then, in later lessons, show students

Planning for Lessons About Prior Knowledge, Initial Observations, and Comparisons

Focus of Lesson	Focus or Investigative Question Stems	Graphic Organizers* * ( ) indicate chapters	Writing Forms or Frames* * ( ) indicate chapters
Accessing prior knowledge	What do you think you know about _____?		Jotting down ideas
Initial observations	What can you observe about _____? What do your senses tell you about _____? What do you observe happening when _____? How can we measure _____? What are some properties/characteristics of _____?	Observations organizer (3, 4, Appendix A) Table (3, 4) System-parts map (3)	Illustrations, diagrams (4) Notetaking (4) Table, map as organizer (3, 4) I observed _____. I noticed _____. Also, _____. In addition, _____. Cause/effect: When I _____, then _____. After _____, then _____.
Compare/contrast	How are _____ and _____ the same (similar) and different?	Box and T-chart (4)	Compare and Contrast frame (4, Appendix A)

FIGURE 7–2 Planning for lessons about prior knowledge, initial observations, and comparisons

how to make and use a table, and sometimes a system-parts map, to guide their observations and thinking (see Chapter 3). In the shared-writing mini-lesson (see Chapter 2), you can model how to use the table or map as a prewriting organizer that guides students in writing detailed observations.

In kindergarten, the initial focus question is connected more specifically with how students will use their senses: "What do your senses tell you about _____ ?" This helps build young students' understanding of senses and how they can use them in discovering characteristics or properties of organisms and objects.

So that your students can learn to record and write about their observations, model during the engagement or reflection stage of the teaching-learning sequence (see Chapter 2) how to make scientific illustrations and diagrams, and take notes in tables (see Chapter 4). Then plan a minilesson in which you model how to use the drawings and tables—along with phrases such as "I observed" and "I noticed"—to write descriptions of what they have observed.

To elicit observations about cause and effect, which is an important part of observing and thinking scientifically, you can use the question "What do you observe happening when _____ ?" During the reflective class discussion and the shared-writing minilesson, you can model using introductory clauses such as "When I" or "After I" to describe causal relationships (see Chapter 4). For example, a kindergartner or first grader might use the clause to write, "When I touched the pillbug, it rolled into a ball." These kinds of frames are remarkably helpful in improving students' abilities to articulate such relationships.

Younger students may need to learn how to use certain tools or techniques to measure something and to understand that using tools is an important part of being a scientist. After students have made some initial observations in a previous lesson, this focus question stem can be useful: "How can we measure _____ ?" In a unit about weather, for instance, the question could be "How can we measure wind speed?"

After a few of these initial lessons, students can begin to describe specific properties or characteristics of the organisms, objects, or events they have been observing. The question "What are some properties/characteristics of _____ ?" focuses students on these scientific terms, which they can begin using now in discussing and writing about what they have observed. (Some units and science standards use the term *properties* in the physical sciences, and *characteristics* in the life and earth/space sciences.)

At some point after observing several different objects or organisms, students will need to compare and contrast them in order to develop a deeper understanding of each one as well as learn the skill of recognizing and organizing similarities and differences (see Chapter 4). A focus question stem for these lessons is "How are _____ and _____ the same (similar) and different?" In your reflective class discussion, you will need to introduce the box and T-chart strategy (see Chapter 4). Then, in the shared-writing minilesson, you can model how to use the Compare and Contrast frame (see Chapter 4 and Appendix A).

As you plan the writing for a unit, be sure you give students enough opportunities to practice the same expository text structures so that they learn how to write them independently. However, be careful not to limit opportunities for students to learn various types of writing. For example, life science units often have a number of lessons in which students can compare and contrast objects or organisms. This strategy is extremely effective, and students and teachers are always excited about how well the students learn to write comparisons. But teachers tend to overdo the use of this strategy and writing frame.

If students already have written two comparisons, you can diversify their writing by using a different type of focus question to introduce the next lesson in which they will be observing different organisms. In writing the question, consider the concepts the students have learned so far, and what question would prompt more critical thinking. For example, "What do you think these organisms need so they can grow and be healthy?" and "What do you think would happen if the terrarium did not have any water?" are questions that require higher-level scientific thinking. Model how to use words from the question to begin a response (for instance, "If the terrarium did not have any water, I think . . . "). Then show students how to provide their reasoning by using this sentence starter: "I think this would happen because . . . "

Lessons About More Focused or Ongoing Observations and Investigations

After the initial lessons of a unit, students become engaged in more focused, and sometimes ongoing, investigations (see Figure 7–3). They have developed greater understanding of some concepts by now and can begin to think about more difficult questions regarding changes over time and cause and effect, for example, and how different parts in a system affect how the entire system functions.

For ongoing investigations in which students are observing changes over time, which is common in life science units, these stems can be useful: "What differences do you observe _____ ?" or "How has _____ changed over time?" or "How has _____ changed since _____ ?" The question "What properties/characteristics affect _____ ?" can engage students in thinking about parts and functions, as well as cause and effect in different systems. Particularly in studies of habitats or ecosystems, you can help students focus on identifying functions of different organisms and the concept of interdependence in ecosystems by using these stems: "What roles do the _____ play in the system?" and "What do you think would happen to the system if _____ ?"

These questions involve more complex thinking than the initial lessons require. Accordingly, you will need to model how to use graphic organizers

Planning for Lessons About More Focused or Ongoing Observations and Investigations

Focus of Lesson	Focus or Investigative Question Stems	Graphic Organizers* * ( ) indicate chapters	Writing Forms or Frames* * ( ) indicate chapters
More focused or ongoing observations	What differences do you observe? How has ____ changed over time? How has ____ changed since ____? What properties affect ____? What roles do the ____ play in the system? What do you think would happen to the system if you ____?	Table (3, 4) T-chart (3, 4, 5)	Illustrations, diagrams (4) Notetaking (4) Table as organizer (4) Use words from question to begin response (4, 5) I noticed ____. I observed ____. In addition, ____. When I ____, then ____. After ____, then ____. At first, ____. But now ____. In the beginning, ____. Now, ____ days later, ____. The evidence is ____. Data Analysis frame (5, Appendix A) Components of a Scientific Conclusion list (5, Appendix A) Useful Words and Phrases (4, Appendix A)
Controlled investigation	What should you consider in planning your investigation about ____? What do you predict will happen and why? What would happen if ____? How does ____ affect ____? What story does the graph tell?	Planning Your Own Scientific Investigation template (3, Appendix A) Data Analysis frame (5, Appendix A)	

FIGURE 7–3 Planning for lessons about more focused or ongoing observations and investigations

and writing frames that will help students organize and communicate about this kind of thinking (see Chapter 5). In the engagement stage of the teaching-learning sequence, model how to make and use tables for recording observations and data. In shared-writing minilessons, show students how to use their tables as organizers for including pertinent data in their explanations and conclusions. For investigations that involve studying changes over time, model using a T-chart during the class discussion so you can help students organize and compare the data from the beginning and end of the investigation. Then, in a writing minilesson, model how to write about the test outcomes by using the T-chart with the frame "At first, _____ . But now, _____ ." This is complex thinking and writing for elementary students, but they can be successful if you use discussions to model the thinking and the organizers, and writing minilessons to model how to use the organizers with writing frames.

In the middle lessons of a unit, if not before, the focus questions also can become investigative questions that are more oriented to planned or controlled investigations. In these lessons, students learn how to plan and conduct fair tests or controlled investigations. A common investigative question stem for such lessons is "What would happen if _____ ?"

An especially effective stem for controlled investigations in the intermediate grades is "How does _____ affect _____ ?" For example, a question that fourth graders investigate in *Land and Water*, a unit published by STC, is "How does greater water flow affect erosion and deposition in the stream system model?" Other, similar questions from this earth science unit are shown in Figure 7–4.

In some lessons, students must learn the skills necessary to plan a fair test or controlled investigation. The focus of the instruction and learning is not the concept, but rather the specific scientific skills and thinking needed to plan a scientific investigation. So the focus question of such a lesson is "What should you consider in planning your investigation about _____ ?" After students have planned the investigation, a typical question they write and respond to in their notebooks is "What do you predict will happen to _____ and why?"

Although students do not need to write their investigation plan (as explained in Chapters 1 and 2), you can model in a class discussion how to plan an investigation by using the Planning Your Own Scientific Investigation template (see Chapter 3 and Appendix A). By doing so, students will learn essential scientific skills, vocabulary, and thinking. If you teach kindergarten or first or second grade, model how to set up what primary students might call a *fair test*. Substitute simple terms for the different variables (for example, "things we need to keep the same" instead of "controlled variables").

In ongoing observations and controlled investigations, students need to learn how to interpret data and provide evidence for their explanations. When they have collected quantitative (measured) data in a previous lesson

---

Focus or Investigative Questions for STC's
Land and Water Unit for Fourth Grade

What do you think you know about land and water?

How can using models help us learn about the real world? Where are all the places water can be on our planet and in your model? How does water change in order to do this?

What happens to land as it rains and where does the rain go?

How does a flowing stream change the land?

What are the properties of each type of soil? How does each soil behave in water?

How does the speed of the water affect the amount of soil that is worn away (eroded) and the amount of soil that is dropped off (deposited)?

What are the similarities and differences of the model streams? What are the common parts of all stream systems?

What patterns do you notice when several streams flow over the land?

How does greater water flow affect the amount of erosion and deposition? What is the evidence from your model that supports your thinking?

How do landforms affect the direction and flow of water?

How do dams affect streams and rivers?

How does sloped land affect the flow of water and the amount of soil that is eroded and deposited downstream?

Where do you predict the water will flow in your landscape? Support your thinking with evidence from past investigations.

If you were to build your landscape and place your homesites again, what would you do differently? Why?

FIGURE 7–4 Focus or investigative questions for *Land and Water* unit

or lessons and have displayed the data in a graph, an important focus question for the lesson is "What story does the graph tell about _____ ?" In class reflective discussions as well as in your shared-writing minilesson, model how to use the Data Analysis frame (see Chapter 5 and Appendix A). Intermediate students also need to use the Components of a Scientific Conclusion list (in Chapter 5 and Appendix A) in organizing their thinking and then writing complex conclusions for their controlled investigations.

Lessons About Application and Connections to the Real World

The last lessons in a unit, and sometimes lessons in the middle, often are oriented toward having students express and apply their summative understanding of the concepts, skills, and thinking in the unit to new challenges (see Figure 7–5). One useful challenge question is "Can you make _____ ?" as in "Can you make a long string make a high pitch?" Another version is "What could you do to _____ ?" For example, in a plant unit, a question might be "What could you do to plants to make them produce more seeds?"

With these types of questions and investigations, you do not need to model using a graphic organizer. During the shared reflection of the science lesson, help students recognize the properties or characteristics they changed and how they think the changes affect how the system works. Then, in the shared-writing minilesson, help scaffold their writing by setting up a type of cause-effect frame: "To make [such and such happen], I _____ . I did this because _____ ."

In some units, students study models—of streams and ecosystems, for example—instead of real systems, just as scientists do. Often in the last lessons, and sometimes earlier, students think and write about the similarities and differences between these models and the actual phenomena. Using the question "How is our model similar and different from _____ ?" frames the lesson. During the shared reflection discussions of this kind of lesson, model how to use the box and T-chart strategy in discussing and organizing the similarities and differences. Then in a shared-writing minilesson, model how to use the graphic organizer and the Compare and Contrast frame (see Chapter 4 and Appendix A) to answer the focus question.

To help students see the relevance of science to their own lives, one or more of the last lessons might focus on the question "How can what we have learned about _____ help us _____ ?" During the shared reflection discussion, you can use a T-chart to organize the students' ideas, then model how to use this frame: "We learned _____ . This can help us when _____ ." For example, in a unit in which students have investigated the properties of different fabrics, they have learned that some materials repel water and some absorb it. They can recognize that this knowledge can help them when they are shopping for a rain jacket and need to determine if the fabric will repel the rain. (Figure 7–6 shows possible focus or investigative questions for *Fabric*, a physical science unit published for kindergartners by FOSS.)

Writing About Focus or Investigative Questions

When students finish a lesson or investigation, they often will write a response in their science notebook to the lesson's focus or investigative question. However, in lessons in which students have not conducted a controlled investigation and have been exploring and observing in a more general or open way, students might benefit from writing about another question. As you plan your instruction, be aware of what students will be learning in a lesson and think carefully about how the writing could deepen their thinking and conceptual understanding. In some cases, students will benefit more from responding to one of the reflective questions in the class discussion. (The teacher's guides can be good sources for these questions.)

Planning for Lessons About Applications and Connections to the Real World

Focus of Lesson	Focus or Investigative Question Stems	Graphic Organizers* * ( ) indicate chapters	Writing Forms or Frames* * ( ) indicate chapters
Application	Can you make [something in particular happen]? What can you do to make [something in particular happen]?		To [make this happen], I ____. I think this worked because ____.
Connections to real world	How is our model similar and different from ____? How can what we have learned about ____ help us ____?	Box and T-chart (4) T-chart (4)	Compare and Contrast frame (4, Appendix A) We learned ____. This can help us when ____. Useful Words and Phrases (4, Appendix A)

FIGURE 7–5 Planning for lessons about applications and connections to the real world

---

Focus or Investigative Questions for the FOSS *Fabric* Unit for Kindergarten

What do your senses tell you about different kinds of fabric?

How are fabrics alike and how are they different?

What do you look for when you are matching different fabrics?

How can you tell if something is made of fabric?

What are some properties of the fabrics that make up a collage?

How do you put pieces of different fabrics together to make a collage?

What is fabric made of? How is some fabric put together?

What can we make when we fasten pieces of fabric together?

What happens to drops of water when you put them on different kinds of fabric?

What is a stain? What can you do to get stains out of fabric?

What do you observe happening when you dip fabric into dye?

What have we learned about the properties of different fabrics?

How can what we have learned about fabric help us in our daily lives?

FIGURE 7–6 Focus or investigative questions for *Fabric* unit

Another option is to provide a different type of writing opportunity. For example, in a lesson in *Plant Growth and Development* (STC), the focus question is "What do the different parts of the bee do?" This is a good question for students to consider as they are observing and learning about bees. But if students write about the question at the end of the lesson, their paragraph will be long and much like a list.

In cases like this, students can get much more out of answering the question by drawing a scientific illustration of a bee, adding labels that name the parts as well as their functions. Near their illustration, students can write a caption that explains something interesting they have learned about bees. Or, if students are learning about the concept of how parts of a system affect its function, then students can write a caption using this frame: "If a bee did not have _____ , then _____ ." In this way, students are using their energy to think and write at a higher level rather than simply writing virtual lists.

Choosing Vocabulary for the Science Word Bank

During the shared reflection stage of a lesson (see Chapter 2), students will have a need to know certain content words. You can anticipate the need for these words and prepare word cards ahead of time. Some units will list words for you, but it is fairly easy to determine the important vocabulary on your own. Remember to add icons, diagrams, or concrete items to the word cards. Also introduce generic science words (for example, *observation*, *data*, and *evidence*). The science word bank section in Chapter 3 provides detailed information about this strategy for developing students' scientific vocabulary.

Successful Planning

Planning the science-writing instruction for a unit is challenging, especially if this is also the first time you have taught the science unit. But keeping these three things in mind will help you be increasingly successful over time:

1. Take time to get a good sense of how concepts and skills are developed through the lessons in a unit. This will help you choose the kinds of focus or investigative questions, graphic organizers, and writing that will support students in developing their understanding, skills, and thinking. (A list of focus and investigative questions for eighteen science units is included in Appendix D.)
2. Use the planning charts in this chapter so you can help your students think and write in increasingly complex ways as the unit progresses.
3. Keep a balance. Do not try to teach too much—elementary students have limited energy and attention spans. But also expect your students to reach higher levels of thinking and writing achievement.

CHAPTER EIGHT

Twelve Tips for Implementing This Integrated Science-Writing Approach

The benefits of implementing this integrated science-writing approach in teaching scientific thinking and writing are well documented in research studies and in hundreds of teachers' testimonials, which also provide some insight into the basic elements of the program that make it effective. The approach is complex, but the following twelve tips will help you recognize and gradually implement these elements over time in your classroom science program.

1. *Teach science and science writing for a minimum of three hours a week*: two sessions of forty-five to sixty minutes for inquiry-based science and two sessions of twenty to thirty minutes for science writing. As stated in Chapter 1, this initially will seem like too much time to incorporate into your full schedule. But hundreds of Seattle teachers would tell you that this investment of time has not only increased their students' achievement in science and expository writing, but also in mathematics, reading, and social studies.

2. *Teach at least one science unit all the way through during the first year you teach with inquiry-based science units.* By investing time so your students experience the complete "story" of a unit, you also increase your students' understanding of science and their scientific thinking and skills. This, in turn, positively affects their expository writing skills. Once you see your students' success, you will want to teach one or two more units. At each grade level, our teachers teach three inquiry-based science units.

3. *Expect students to use science notebooks in every science session.* Provide bound notebooks with lined paper so students have plenty of lined space for their writing. (Kindergartners use notebooks with plain white pages.) Students should write the date, a focus question, and at least a

few sentences about their observations and thinking (not the procedures) in every lesson. They also should write data and observation notes in their notebooks, and refer to them during class discussions.

4. *Provide a focus or investigative question for each lesson* to focus students' minds on a question about the main concept, thinking, and/or scientific skill that students will develop through their experiences in the lesson.

5. *Teach students to use the word* because *in their discussions and notebook entries.* This will help them remember to provide reasoning and evidence for their thinking.

6. *Use a science word bank.* Introduce new terms on word cards *after* students have had a concrete experience and have a need to know the new vocabulary. Make this word bank an integral part of your science discussions.

7. *Teach students how to construct and use graphic organizers*, starting with simple tables and T-charts. These visual structures will help students organize and develop their thinking and writing.

8. *Use writing frames in your shared-writing minilessons.* Begin with simple frames such as "I observed" and "I think _____ because _____." Add new structures as the unit progresses.

9. *Model everything: scientific skills, critical thinking, how to write different types of notebook entries, and so on.* Engage students in this modeling—as in the shared-writing minilesson—rather than just talking at them or having them simply copy something you have put on the board.

10. *Assess notebooks as rough drafts.* Analyze entries in terms of conceptual understanding, scientific thinking, and scientific skills, and the writing traits of content, organization, and word choice. Do *not* assess neatness or handwriting (unless it is illegible), conventions (spelling, punctuation, and grammar), sentence fluency, or voice. Students turn their full attention to these traits only if they edit and publish the notebook entries in a finished, formal way later on.

11. *Provide positive constructive feedback.* Start with specific strengths. If an entry is unclear, inaccurate, or missing something, ask a student a question about it from a scientist's point of view: "If another scientist were reading this, what would he or she need to know about . . . ?" If the student struggles with writing, note only the strengths. Never score the notebooks. With positive, unscored feedback—and meaningful things to write about with structured support that helps them be successful—even reluctant writers enjoy making entries in their science notebooks.

12. *Expect that your students can do more than you think they can.* When you provide ongoing modeling of the skills, scaffolding for the thinking and writing, meaningful opportunities to think and write independently, and positive, constructive feedback, your students will progress beyond where you, or they, ever thought they could go.

Getting Started

Because of the complexity of this science-writing approach, you will not be able to implement everything at once. In hundreds of testimonials over the years, most of our teachers say that they focused on the following components of the approach when they were getting started:

1. Encourage students to use *because* to provide their reasoning and thinking, both in science discussions and in their writing.
2. Use a focus or investigative question in every science session.
3. Develop and use a science word bank in science discussions and writing sessions.
4. Create and use simple graphic organizers such as the box and T-chart for making comparisons.
5. Provide simple writing frames to scaffold students' writing.

After our teachers had taught one or more units, most said that they began to incorporate some more complex components:

1. Respond thoughtfully and constructively to students' notebook entries.
2. Emphasize the strengths in an entry based on what other scientists would appreciate.
3. Ask students questions that will lead them to improve the entry based on what their scientific audience might need to know.
4. Develop better modeling skills, which includes moving students away from relying on writing frames by engaging them in writing entries in different ways.

Above all, as you begin to implement this science-writing approach, *be patient with yourself*. Our teachers generally feel confident about their instruction after they have taught a science unit, including the science writing, for three years. Based on the experiences of these teachers, you can expect, as you become more comfortable teaching in these ways, to see unexpected growth in your students' scientific skills, thinking, and understanding. Unconsciously you will create an exciting scientific atmosphere in your classroom. When students feel your excitement about their thinking and their work, believe that they are scientists working together to make discoveries, and see that their notebooks are tools and important ways of communicating with other scientists, they will love doing scientific investigations and writing about their thinking and understanding. Hundreds of teachers and students in Seattle's Science Notebooks Program can testify that this is what happened to them. One student spoke for them all in saying, "A good day is when we do science!"

Appendix A *Blackline Masters for Graphic Organizers and Writing Frames*

A–1   Teaching and Learning of Science and Scientific Writing

A–2   Science Session: The Teaching-Learning Sequence and Students' Use of Science Notebooks

A–3   Writing Session: Shared-Writing Minilesson and Independent Writing

A–4   Planning Your Own Scientific Investigation

A–5   Observations

A–6   Compare and Contrast

A–7   Useful Words and Phrases in Scientific Writing

A–8   Components of a Scientific Conclusion

A–9   Data Analysis

A–10 Criteria for Exemplary Science Notebook Entries

A–11 Assessing Student Work and Planning Instruction

A–12 Science-Writing Reflection Groups: Protocol for Instructional Planning Meetings

A–13 Science-Writing Reflection Groups: Protocol for Assessing Notebook Entries

A–14 Notes About Lessons Learned

A–15 Planning for Lessons About Prior Knowledge, Initial Observations, and Comparisons

A–16 Planning for Lessons About More Focused or Ongoing Observations and Investigations

A–17 Planning for Lessons About Applications and Connections to the Real World

Teaching and Learning of Science and Scientific Writing

Science Session	Science-Writing Session
Through inquiry, students learn:	*Using their science experiences and understanding as the content of their writing, students learn different forms of scientific writing, including:*
■ science content—concepts and principles, or "big ideas" ■ scientific thinking—critical reasoning, problem solving ■ scientific skills—for example, observing, conducting investigations, using data	■ observations ■ cause and effect ■ comparisons ■ reasoning ■ data analysis ■ conclusions
Science notebooks:	*Science notebooks:*
■ used for observation notes, illustrations, data ■ provide evidence for discussions	■ used for writing that communicates higher levels of scientific thinking and conceptual understanding
Scaffolding:	*Scaffolding:*
■ scientific inquiry ■ word banks ■ graphic organizers	■ word banks ■ graphic organizers ■ writing frames

Science Session: The Teaching-Learning Sequence and Students' Use of Science Notebooks

Stages	1. Engagement	2. Active Investigation	3. Shared Reflection	4. Application
Teacher	Models making tables, notes, data entries, illustrations, diagrams.	Works with groups: ■ asks questions ■ models language, thinking ■ addresses misconceptions.	Models making tables, graphs of class data, graphic organizers. Introduces new words to word bank. Models language, thinking.	Leads discussion to connect lesson with real world or further investigations.
Students	Write: ■ date ■ focus or investigative question ■ prediction with reasoning ■ table.	Record data. Take notes. Make illustrations, diagrams.	Use notebooks to provide data for class results, evidence for own reasoning, explanations, conclusions.	May use notebooks to provide ideas, questions.

Writing Session: Shared-Writing Minilesson and Independent Writing

Steps	1. Shared Review	2. Shared Writing	3. Scaffolding	4. Independent Writing
Teacher	Questions students about shared reflection of conclusions from previous science session.	Models structure of specific writing form (e.g., comparison, conclusion).	Writes scaffolding for notebook entry (e.g., sentence starters, phrases, words).	Works with small groups or individuals who need extra support or more challenges. Asks questions, models language, rereads writing with students.
Students	Provide reflections, explanations.	Provide content of the writing.		Use scaffolding as they write their own notebook entries.

Planning Your Own Scientific Investigation

Use this form when you want to design and conduct your own investigation of a question that you and your group want to explore.

Investigative question (the question you want to investigate). Include both the changed (manipulated) variable and the measured/observed (responding) variable.

Prediction, including your reasoning. (You might write, *I predict* _____ *because* _____ .) Include the variable you will change and what you will measure/observe.

Procedure

List the one changed (manipulated) variable:	List the most important logical steps; include all the different variables and their amounts:
List the variables you will keep the same or constant (controlled variables):	
	List the most important materials:

List the variable you will measure and/or observe (measured/observed or responding variable):

How often and/or how many times will you measure and/or observe it?

Make a table for recording the data.
Repeat the tests/procedure at least 3 times.

After you have completed the investigation and talked with your group about the results, *write a conclusion.* Answer the *question that you have been investigating*, providing the data (results of your investigation) as *evidence of your thinking.* Also write about whether or not the results of the investigation support your *prediction.* If necessary, you might also explain what you think caused *inconclusive or inconsistent data* in your results (consider the *variables* in your tests).

Observations

Think of the four senses (not taste).	Size, shape, color, lines, patterns, texture, weight, smell/odor, sound, behavior . . .
	I observed _____ .
	I noticed _____ .
Connect it with what you know or have investigated.	It reminds me of _____ because _____ .
Observe and record cause and effect.	When _____ , it _____ .
Note any changes.	At first, _____ . But now _____ .
Be curious, and ask questions you might investigate.	I am curious about _____ . It surprised me that _____ because _____ .
	I wonder what would happen if _____ .
	How does _____ affect _____ ?

Compare and Contrast

Start with how things are the same or similar.

The _____ and the _____ are similar because they both _____ . In addition, they _____ .

Add more as needed.

. . .

Explain how they are different. You can compare the same property or characteristic in the same sentence. Use *and, but,* or *whereas* to set up the contrast.

They are different because the _____ , but the _____ . Also, the _____ , whereas _____ .

Add more as needed.

. . .

Remember to ask, "Will it be clear to the reader what I mean when I use pronouns such as *they* and *it*? If not, how can I edit the sentence to make it clearer?"

Useful Words and Phrases in Scientific Writing

Questions	Observations	Contrasts	Sequence of Time, Cause and Effect, Reasoning
What would happen if _____? How does [*the changed variable*] affect [*the measured, observed, responding variable*]?	I observed I noticed When _____, After _____,	_____, but _____. _____ whereas _____. However, In contrast, At first, _____. But now, _____.	First, _____. Next, _____. Then, _____. Finally, _____. If _____, then _____. So, This leads to As a result, Consequently,

Evidence	Reasoning	Adding Information, Evidence, Reasoning	Conclusions
_____ because _____. For example, For instance, The evidence is The data show The data provide evidence that	_____ because _____. I think this because I think this means	Also, In addition, Furthermore,	Therefore, I think In conclusion, I think Therefore, In conclusion,

Note to teachers: Students can become too dependent on sentence starters and writing frames that teachers provide. To support students in becoming more independent writers, you can post a chart like this in the classroom, adding words and phrases as needed. Also teach students to use words from questions as appropriate in beginning their responses.

Components of a Scientific Conclusion

- **Answer the investigative question in a general way,** using the words from the question in your answer if possible: What happens to the brightness of a bulb when you change the length of wire in a closed circuit? "When I change the length of wire in a closed circuit, the brightness of the bulb changes."

- **Provide evidence from your observations or tests.** *Include:*

  Qualitative data (for example, *more/less; longer/shorter; brighter/dimmer*): "The bulb was brighter with shorter wire and dimmer with longer wire."

  Quantitative data (measured data): "For example, with 10 cm wire, the bulb brightness was 9. But with the 30 cm wire, the brightness was only 7."

- **Make a concluding statement(s) that is based on the evidence:** "Therefore, the shortest wire makes the bulb the brightest and the longest wire makes the bulb the dimmest."

- **Refer to your prediction.** Did your data support it? If they did not, how has your thinking changed? "The data did not support my prediction because I thought that the bulbs would have the same brightness. I didn't think the length of the wire would make any difference. Now I know that the length does have an effect."

- **Make an inference about what you think caused these test results:** "I think this happens because longer wire has more resistance than shorter wire."

- **If you had data that were different from what other groups had, what do you think could have caused these results?** "I think my group got different results because we used a different type of wire than the others did. We should have kept that variable the same as everyone else."

- **What other questions do you have now that you want to investigate?** "What would happen if we used wires of different thicknesses?"

Data Analysis

Start with a topic sentence to say what the graph / table is about (as shown in the main title and the title for each axis/row or column).

This graph / table shows _____ .

Summarize the data. (Write about the important points in the graph or table; do *not* write about all the data.)

- *Qualitative* data (e.g., *more/fewer*; *increase/ decrease*)

The larger wheels go *farther* than the smaller wheels do.

The distance *increases* as the wheels get larger.

- Specific *quantitative* data (e.g., actual numbers, percentages) Give examples from the greatest and least; *do not include all the data in between.*

For example, the 4.5 cm wheels went *145 cm*, whereas the 11 cm wheels went *276 cm*.

End with a conclusion that answers the question you were investigating (investigative question). Include:

- The main *inferences* made from the data.

Therefore, I think _____ .

- Whether the data support your *prediction* and if your thinking has changed.

The data _____ . My thinking _____ .

You may also need to include:

- *Outliers* and *inconsistent* or *inconclusive data* and what you think might have caused them (e.g., variables in the testing).

Some data were inconsistent. I think this happened because _____ .

- How this information might be important in the real world.

This information could be important _____ because _____ .

Criteria for Exemplary Science Notebook Entries

Conceptual Understanding	Scientific Skills and Thinking	Expository Writing
Understanding of "big ideas" of unit Demonstrates, through words and graphics, an accurate and quite full grasp of the major science concepts that were introduced ********************************* May demonstrate one or more of the following: ■ Appropriately/accurately applies previous learning to new concepts and skills ■ Extends the new concept or skill to new problems or new phenomena	*Use of scientific inquiry skills* Thorough and purposeful use of skills to advance learning. For example: ■ Makes accurate and full observations, with complete records ■ Collects and records data accurately, completely, and honestly ■ Examines data and identifies results (for example, by comparing different data points) ■ Shows understanding of fair tests or controlled investigations *Use of evidence to support explanations* Demonstrates understanding of relationship between data and explanation: ■ Supports explanations with appropriate data *Use of critical thinking skills to draw inferences* Demonstrates understanding of relationships between data and inference: ■ Draws reasonable inferences from data; supports inferences with reasoning	*Idea/content (development)* Has control of content: ■ States information or idea clearly ■ Develops information or idea fully with relevant details, evidence, and explanation *Organization (sequence)* ■ Uses different text structures to organize ideas/information effectively ■ Logically sequences or groups details ■ Uses appropriate transition words to show logical connections *Word choice* ■ Uses scientific vocabulary accurately ■ Uses nonscientific vocabulary effectively to clarify and explain ********************************* These traits *may* be apparent: *Voice (authority)* ■ Has an engaged voice that shows confidence with scientific stance ■ May include self-reflection *Sentence fluency (sentence structure and variety)* ■ Can use multiple types of clauses and structures to clarify and develop ideas

Adaptation of chart by Inverness Research Associates, July 2002.

Assessing Student Work and Planning Instruction

1. Look briefly at each entry prior to the one you are assessing to give you a general idea of the quality of the student's entries.
2. Before assessing the selected entry, think about the:
   - science concept(s)/"big idea(s)" of the lesson/investigation and how it (they) related to the development of concepts in the unit;
   - scientific skills and thinking that may be involved in the lesson/investigation;
   - important structures and language in the expository writing;
   - question(s) to which the student may be responding in the entry.
3. Follow the Criteria for Exemplary Science Notebook Entries chart as you assess the entry.
   - Skim the entry. Then reread it carefully, considering each of these criteria. (Do *not* consider other criteria.)
   - *Note strengths of each component first*, then weaknesses. Determine further instruction for student or class.
   - Write constructive feedback on a sticky note and place it on the entry.

Strengths	Weaknesses	Further Instruction

Science-Writing Reflection Groups
Protocol for Instructional Planning Meetings

The facilitator's role is to ensure that the protocol is followed.

For each lesson you are planning:

1. Reflect about the *"big ideas"/concepts* of the lesson and how they relate to the development of concepts throughout the unit.
2. Consider the *scientific skills and thinking* that may be involved in the investigation.
3. Think about the *expository writing skills* students will need in order to communicate their understanding and thinking in the lesson.
4. Consider the lesson's *focus/investigative question(s) and/or the reflective question(s)* to which the students may be responding in the entry.
5. Discuss the *challenges* students could face in terms of points 1 through 4.
6. Determine *what the teacher will need to model* before the lesson and/or the writing.

At the end of the meeting, plan what student work each teacher will bring to the next meeting.

Unit Title _____   Date _____

Lesson	Notes

Science-Writing Reflection Groups
Protocol for Instructional Planning Meetings *(Continued)*

Unit Title _____   Date _____

Lesson	Notes

Science-Writing Reflection Groups
Protocol for Assessing Notebook Entries

The facilitator's role is to ensure that the protocol is followed.

1. Consider the specific concepts, scientific skills and thinking, and expository writing that pertain to the selected lesson and entry.
2. Briefly go over the Criteria for Exemplary Science Notebook Entries chart, which presents the general standards we expect students to meet in the notebook entries. Discuss the criteria in terms of the entry you will be assessing.
3. Silently, and fairly quickly, read through the first student sample without looking for anything in particular.

   ■ The teacher who provides the sample should *not* explain anything about the student or the entry.

4. Read the entry again, focusing on only the strengths in terms of the criteria.
5. Discuss the *strengths* of the sample:

   ■ Do *not* mention any weaknesses.
   ■ Do *not* discuss any other criteria (e.g., neatness, conventions—spelling, punctuation, grammar).
   ■ List the strengths on the Assessing Student Work and Planning Instruction form. All teachers can do this, or one teacher can volunteer to record these notes for the teacher whose student's entry is being assessed.

6. Discuss the *weaknesses* of the sample in terms of the criteria.

   ■ List the weaknesses on the assessment form.

7. Discuss and plan further instruction and feedback that could build on the strengths and improve the weaknesses.

   ■ Make notes on the form regarding further instruction.

8. Give a completed form to the teacher whose student's entry was assessed.

Notes About Lessons Learned

Unit Title _____ *Date* _____

Lesson	Notes—Lessons Learned About Content, Pedagogy, Writing, Modeling, etc.

Planning for Lessons About Prior Knowledge, Initial Observations, and Comparisons

Focus of Lesson	Focus or Investigative Question Stems	Graphic Organizers* * ( ) indicate chapters	Writing Forms or Frames* * ( ) indicate chapters
Accessing prior knowledge	What do you think you know about ____?		Jotting down ideas
Initial observations	What can you observe about ____? What do your senses tell you about ____? What do you observe happening when ____? How can we measure ____? What are some properties/characteristics of ____?	Observations organizer (3, 4, Appendix A) Table (3, 4) System-parts map (3)	Illustrations, diagrams (4) Notetaking (4) Table, map as organizer (3, 4) I observed ____. I noticed ____. Also, ____. In addition, ____. Cause/effect: When I ____, then ____. After ____, then ____.
Compare/contrast	How are ____ and ____ the same (similar) and different?	Box and T-chart (4)	Compare and Contrast frame (4, Appendix A)

Planning for Lessons About More Focused or Ongoing Observations and Investigations

Focus of Lesson	Focus or Investigative Question Stems	Graphic Organizers* * ( ) indicate chapters	Writing Forms or Frames* * ( ) indicate chapters
More focused or ongoing observations	What differences do you observe? How has _____ changed over time? How has _____ changed since _____? What properties affect _____ ? What roles do the _____ play in the system? What do you think would happen to the system if you _____ ?	Table (3, 4) T-chart (3, 4, 5)	Illustrations, diagrams (4) Notetaking (4) Table as organizer (4) Use words from question to begin response (4, 5) I noticed _____ . I observed _____ . In addition, _____ . When I _____ , then _____ . After _____ , then _____ .
Controlled investigation	What should you consider in planning your investigation about _____ ? What do you predict will happen and why? What would happen if _____ ? How does _____ affect _____ ? What story does the graph tell?	Planning Your Own Scientific Investigation template (3, Appendix A) Data Analysis frame (5, Appendix A)	At first, _____ . But now _____ . In the beginning, _____ . Now, _____ days later, _____ . The evidence is _____ . Data Analysis frame (5, Appendix A) Components of a Scientific Conclusion list (5, Appendix A) Useful Words and Phrases (4, Appendix A)

Planning for Lessons About Applications and Connections to the Real World

Focus of Lesson	Focus or Investigative Question Stems	Graphic Organizers* * ( ) indicate chapters	Writing Forms or Frames* * ( ) indicate chapters
Application	Can you make [something in particular happen]? What can you do to make [something in particular happen]?		To [make this happen], I _____. I think this worked because _____.
Connections to real world	How is our model similar and different from _____? How can what we have learned about _____ help us _____?	Box and T-chart (4) T-chart (4)	Compare and Contrast frame (4, Appendix A) We learned _____. This can help us when _____. Useful Words and Phrases (4, Appendix A)

© 2007 by Betsy Rupp Fulwiler from *Writing in Science*. Portsmouth, NH: Heinemann.

Appendix B *A First Grader's Complete Science Notebook*

In the spring of first grade, Symphony and her classmates have been studying *Balls and Ramps*, a physical science unit published by Insights. Her notebook reveals much of what she has learned about science concepts, scientific thinking and skills, and scientific writing through her experiences in the unit. The entries also illustrate some of the instructional strategies her teacher uses to scaffold his students' learning. About 25 percent of his students are served in the ELL program and about 75 percent receive free or reduced-price lunch.

Symphony's completed science notebook is shown on the following pages, with captions to describe what the teacher and the class did before students began writing each notebook entry. Because it is spring and this is the students' third science unit of the year, the routines and habits of scientific learning are already established in the classroom. Elementary students in Seattle Public Schools receive science notebooks as part of the K–5 Inquiry-Based Science Program.

Science Notebook

SEATTLE
PUBLIC
SCHOOLS

Name Symphony

Grade 1

On April 19, the teacher and students construct a class chart of observations they have made about different kinds of balls. In the shared-writing mini-lesson, the teacher models how to use the chart as an organizer for writing a description of a ball. Symphony chooses to write about a basketball and uses the chart to decide what she wants to include in her writing.

4-19-05

How can you describe different balls?

Basketball

The Basketball is a Sphere and it has brown and it is rough it has air

On April 20, the class observes two balls, then their teacher does a minilesson on using the box and T-chart to compare the two. Then he models how to use the Compare and Contrast frame (as explained in Chapter 4) for writing a comparison about them. The next day, the students observe two other balls and repeat the minilesson. Finally, they write their own comparison in their notebook under the date and focus question they had entered in their notebook the day before.

4-20-05

How are (balls) the (same) and how are they (different?)

The Rubber Ball and the
Ping Pong Ball are the same
because both are Sphere.
In addition they both
roll win you roll it fast.
They are different
because the Rubber Ball
is Shiny and the Ping Pong
Ball is dull. Also the
Rubber Ball is made out
of Rubber. but the Ping
Pong Ball is made out of Plastic.

The students explore the properties of additional balls on April 22 and continue to fill out the class properties chart. Next, they conduct an investigation of four specific properties shown in the data table. They test a rubber ball ("R") and a polystyrene ball ("P") and record the results of their tests in their notebooks.

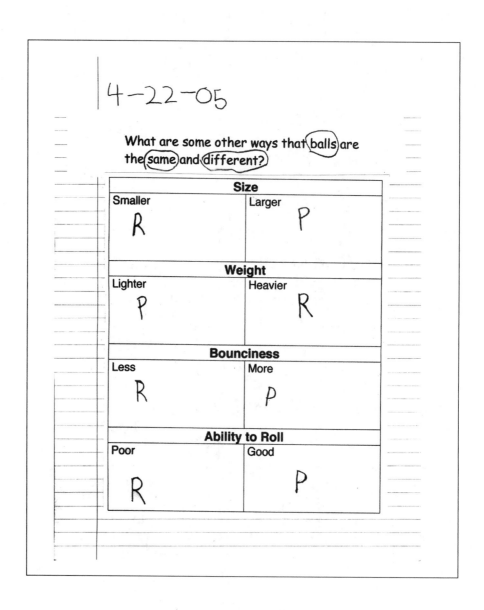

4-22-05

What are some other ways that balls are the same and different?

Size	
Smaller	Larger
R	P

Weight	
Lighter	Heavier
P	R

Bounciness	
Less	More
R	P

Ability to Roll	
Poor	Good
R	P

On April 25, students briefly investigate how different balls roll. They write a class definition of a good roller: "A good roller rolls straight and far. It is smooth with no bumps." Then students write about which balls they observed were the best rollers and what properties they think made them good rollers.

4-25-05

The best rollers are the Rubber ball and the wooden ball. I think this because they both have no bumps and they both roll straight.

On April 26, the teacher addresses his students' misconceptions about the meaning of *hard* and *heavy* by guiding them in further explorations with the balls. The next day, he asks them to write answers to three questions, each of which he writes on the overhead in a different color to make them easy to distinguish. Students use the words of the questions independently in writing their answers, which is evident in Symphony's entry.

4-26-05

Which (balls) are (easier) and (harder) to (start) (moving?)

The Ping Pong Ball was easier to start moving because it is light. The marble was harder to move because it is heavy. The marble could knock over the glue bottle because it is heavy.

On April 29, students independently write an observation of one ball as an embedded assessment of what they have learned about making scientific observations and writing about them. (This entry is analyzed in Chapter 6.)

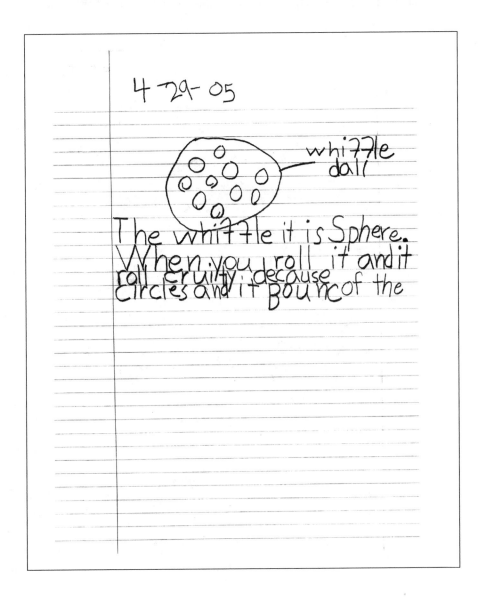

By May 2, students have had many experiences with different balls and clearly understand which balls are the good bouncers. So their teacher focuses their thinking and writing on the properties they infer might be causing the balls to be good bouncers. He writes *I think* and *because* on the overhead next to the focus question to remind students of what they need to state and explain.

5-2-05

What kinds of (balls) are (good) (bouncers?)

I think the Rubber
Ball is a good bouncers
because. It is Solid and I
Odserved the Rubber
Ball that it is made.
Out of Rubber.

Students have collected and recorded their data in their T-charts on May 4. They circle the "middle number" of their data for each ball, write the numbers on different colored sticky notes, then place the notes on the appropriate places on the class graph of their test results. After a shared-writing minilesson about writing scientific conclusions, the teacher provides the following scaffolding for their writing:

- I think _____ because _____
- My evidence _____

Symphony does not complete this notebook entry. Also note that she is reporting about the cumulative class results rather than about the data in her T-charts. Students know that the class data represent many more trials than what they do in one group.

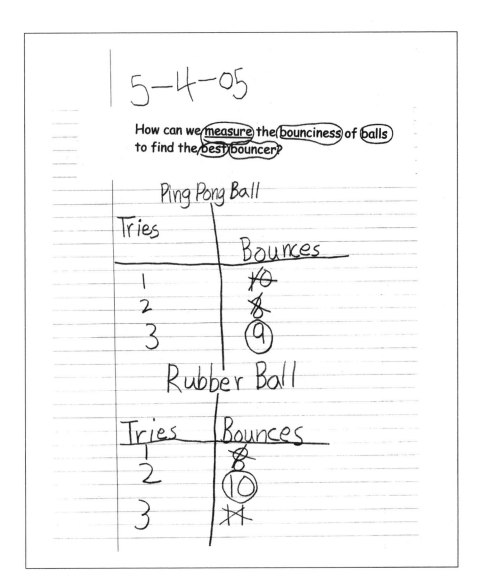

And the   the pingpong
Ball bounces more time
then the Rubber and

Students were confused in the last science session about how to write about their data. So on May 10, after more discussion and modeling of the writing, their teacher provides this scaffolding:

I noticed	more
	less
My evidence is	data
I think	better
	worse
	the same

Symphony responds with the first-grade equivalent of a scientific conclusion.

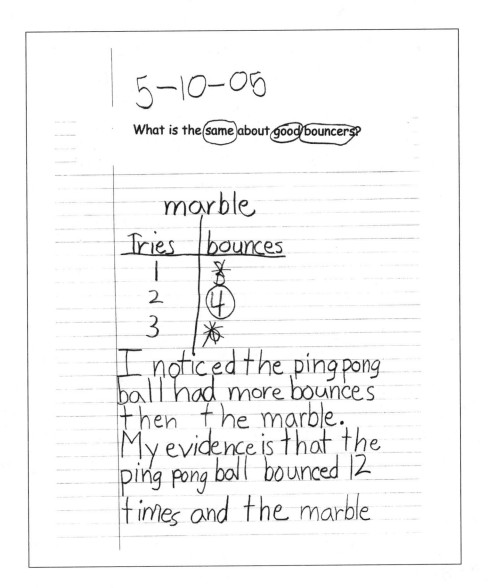

bounced 4 times. And I think the ping pong ball is a good bouncer and I think the marble isa bad bouncer.

By this time of the unit, on May 11, students begin to think about how to apply what they have learned about the properties of balls as they make their own balls out of classroom materials. Their teacher asks them to write about three questions as they think about their design plans:

- What are you going to make it out of?
- What do you want it to look like?
- What do you want it to be able to do?

Symphony addresses two of the three questions in her entry.

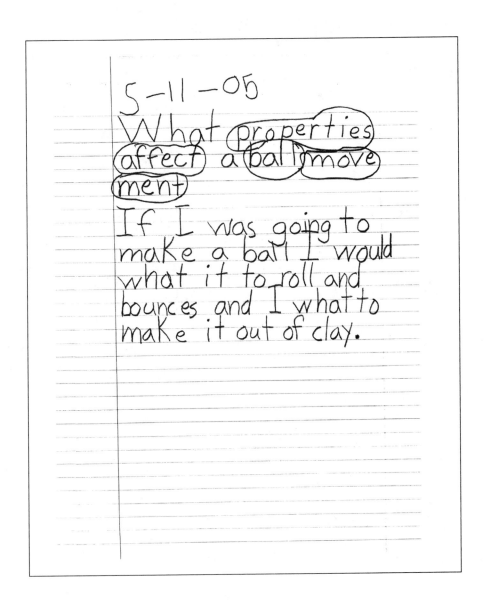

On May 16, students are to draw and label a ramp system. Part of what they are investigating is how parts in a system have functions that affect how the whole system works.

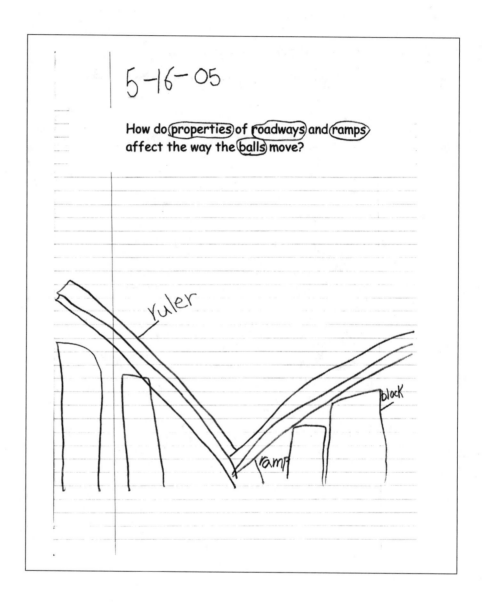

5-16-05

How do (properties) of (roadways) and (ramps) affect the way the (balls) move?

ruler

block

ramp

On May 18, after a shared review of the results of their tests of the investigative question, students write independently in their notebooks using this scaffolding:

I noticed	more
	less
My evidence is	data
I think	Why do you think the ball moved the block
	more on a 2-block ramp?

Symphony has recorded the results of her group's tests in her notebook, but she writes about the cumulative results from all the group tests. Her entry, like many others from throughout the district, indicates that the focus question for this lesson does not help students think clearly about the different aspects of their investigation outcomes. Students now respond to these two focus questions: How does the steepness of the ramp affect the speed of a ball? How does the speed of a ball affect how far a ball moves an object?

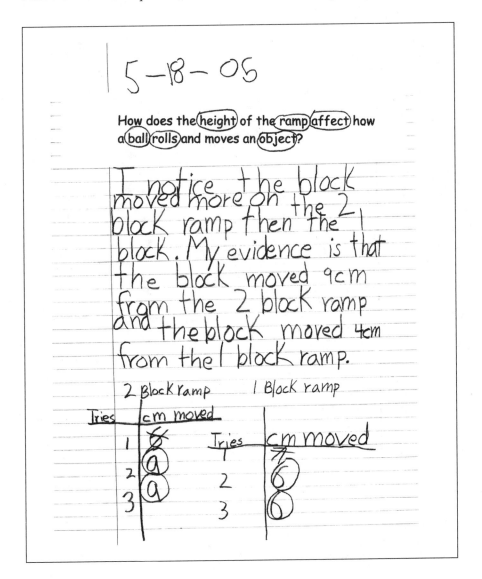

I think the ball went
fast on the 2 block ramp
because it had 2 blocks and
it is steeper.

On May 23, students have investigated the question by using a marble and a rubber ball. They have recorded the results of each group's tests. Their teacher provides this scaffolding for the independent writing time:

- Answer using the focus question
- Evidence from the T-chart
- *Therefore*
- What did you learn about balls that are different sizes?

Symphony writes her conclusion based on the class data.

5-23-50

Do balls of different sizes roll down the ramp at different speeds or the same speed?

Speed of 2 balls

Tie	No Tie
ﬀﬀﬀ	|||

The rubberball and the marble rolled down the ramp at the Same time. My evidence is the rubber ball and the marble tied 33 times it didn't tie 16 time. I lean it dost mater what sies the ball are it still rolls the same speed.

At the end of the unit, on June 1, students are investigating the effect of weight on the speed of the balls. The teacher provides similar scaffolding as he did for the previous entry:

- What did you learn about balls of different weights?
- Evidence
- *Therefore*

This is Symphony's response (which is analyzed in Chapter 6).

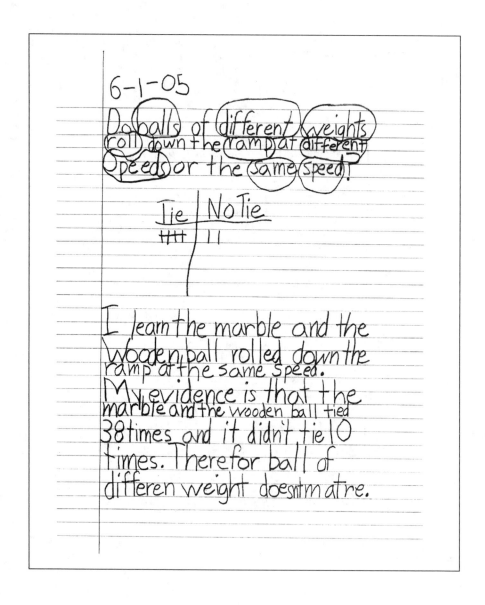

The photo shows Symphony as a second grader, making an entry in a new science notebook. The teacher loops with his students from first to second grade. Symphony has become one of the star scientists in the classroom.

Appendix C   *Resources for Inquiry-Based Science Units*

FOSS (Full Option Science System) Science Units

Developer: FOSS Project Site, Lawrence Hall of Science, Berkeley, California. www.lawrencehallofscience.org/foss/.

Vendor: Delta Education. www.delta-education.com/.

Insights Science Units

Developer: Education Development Center, Inc. http://main.edc.org/.

Vendor: Kendall Hunt Publishing Company. www.kendallhunt.com/.

STC (Science and Technology for Children) Science Units

Developer: National Science Resources Center. www.nsrconline.org/curriculum_resources/index.html.

Vendor: Carolina Biological. www2.carolina.com/webapp/wcs/stores/servlet/StoreCatalogDisplay? storeld=10151&catalogld=10101&langld=-1.

Appendix D *Focus and Investigative Questions for Inquiry-Based Science Units*

In Seattle's K–5 Inquiry-Based Science Program and the Science Notebooks Program, we have developed focus and investigative questions for all our science units. The questions are included in this appendix. Please note that some questions are for lessons that we have added to the units, with the help of scientists, to meet our state science standards. The grade levels are the grades in which we teach the units to our students.

Animals Two by Two (FOSS)—Kindergarten

What do you notice about the body of the goldfish?

How do goldfish behave? How do they behave when new things are placed in their space?

How does goldfish behavior change when a new object is placed in the aquarium?

What do you notice about the body and behavior of the platys?

How are the platys and the goldfish the same and different?

What do you notice about the body of the land snails? How do land snails behave and move?

What foods do land snails eat?

What do you think can change the way land snails behave and move?

What do you notice about the body of the water snail?

How are land snails and water snails alike and how are they different?

Do land snails spend more time on rough or smooth surfaces?

What do you notice about the body of the earthworms?

How do earthworms behave and move? How did they react when they came to a barrier in their path?

Do earthworms spend more time on moist or dry soil?

What do you notice about the body and behavior of the night crawlers?

How are red worms and night crawlers alike and how are they different? What basic needs do both kinds of worms have in order to stay alive?

What do you notice about the body and behavior of the isopods?

How are the pillbugs and sowbugs alike and how are they different?

Do isopods move to open, lighted places or sheltered, dark places?

What do you think fish, snails, earthworms, and isopods need in order to live and be healthy?

Fabric (FOSS)—Kindergarten

What do your senses tell you about different kinds of fabric?

How are fabrics alike and how are they different?

What do you look for when you are matching different fabrics?

How can you tell if something is made of fabric?

What are some properties of the fabrics that make up a collage?

How do you put pieces of different fabrics together to make a collage?

What is fabric made of? How is some fabric put together?

What can we make when we fasten pieces of fabric together?

What happens to drops of water when you put them on different kinds of fabric?

What is a stain? What can you do to get stains out of fabric?

What do you observe happening when you dip fabric into dye?

What have we learned about the properties of different fabrics?

How can what we have learned about fabric help us in our daily lives?

Wood (FOSS)—Kindergarten

What do your senses tell you about different kinds of wood? How are different kinds of wood alike and different?

What do you look for when you match different kinds of wood? How can you tell whether something is made of wood?

What happens when you put drops of water on different kinds of wood?

What happens when you put wood in water? How can you make different kinds of wood sink to the bottom of the tub of water? What do you observe when you try to sink different kinds of wood?

How many paper clips does it take to sink the cedar and particleboard?

How does sanding the wood change it?

How are sawdust and shavings alike and different? What happens to sawdust and shavings when you put them in water?

How is particleboard made?

How is plywood made?

How can two pieces of wood be joined together?

How does staining the wood change it?

How can wood be joined together to make useful or beautiful structures?

Balls and Ramps (Insights)—First Grade

How can you describe different balls?

How are balls similar and different?

What are some other ways balls are similar and different?

Which balls are easier and harder to start moving?

What kinds of balls are good bouncers?

How can we measure the bounciness of balls to find the best bouncer?

What is the same about good bouncers?

What properties affect a ball's movement?

What materials can be used to make balls? How should balls be constructed so they can roll and bounce?

How do properties of roadways and ramps affect the way balls move?

How does the steepness of the ramp affect the speed of a ball? How does the speed of a ball affect how far a ball moves an object?

Do balls of different weights roll down the ramp at different speeds or the same speed?

Do balls of different sizes roll down the ramp at different speeds or the same speed?

How can you control the behavior of the balls when you build a ramp system?

Organisms (STC)—First Grade

What do living things need in order to stay alive?

What can we observe about different seeds?

What do seeds need to live and grow?

Do seeds (and plants) need light in order to grow and be healthy?

What do you observe about woodland plants?

How are the hornwort and the duckweed similar and different?

How have our seeds changed?

What do our senses tell us about the snails' bodies and behaviors?

How are cloud fish and snails alike and different?

What do you observe about the isopods?

Do isopods need moist or dry soil in their habitat?

What are the characteristics and behaviors of the mystery animals [mealworm beetle larvae]? How are the isopods and the mystery animals similar and different?

How do you think the mystery animals may change in the next few weeks?

What changes are you observing in the aquarium?

What changes are you noticing in the terrarium?

How are freshwater and woodland plants alike and different?

How are freshwater and woodland animals alike and different?

How are plants and animals alike and different?

How are humans similar to and different from plants and animals? What do all organisms need to live and be healthy?

Weather (STC)—First Grade

What is the weather like today? How does the weather affect what we wear and what we do?

What can our senses tell us about the weather?

How can we tell how much the wind is blowing?

How can we record the weather? How does the weather change from day to day and through the seasons?

What do the numbers on the thermometer tell us about the temperature?

Is the temperature inside the room the same as or different from the temperature outside?

How are clouds alike and different? How can we identify clouds?

When hot and cold water are mixed together, what is the temperature of the mixed water?

In sunlight, would we feel warmer, cooler, or the same if we wore black clothes or white clothes?

How can we keep track of how much rain falls each day?

What can we observe over time about water in a puddle?

Which fabrics can keep us driest in the rain?

What do you think meteorologists should observe when they forecast the weather? How was the weather forecast for today similar to and different from the actual weather?

Balancing and Weighing (STC)—Second Grade

What do we know about balancing?

What do you have to do to balance something?

What do you have to do to balance the beam?

Where did you need to place the heavier weight to balance the beam?

How do you balance a mobile?

How are an equal-arm balance and a beam balance similar and different?

How can an equal-arm balance help you compare objects?

What are some strategies you might use to place the objects in serial order?

How are balancing and weighing alike?

How do graphs give us a clear picture of the weight of objects?

What do you notice about each food when you observe it carefully?

What do you know about the properties of the pieces of food that might help you in predicting the weight of a cupful of food?

What do the line plots tell us about the weight of the foods?

Why do you think foods that weigh the same take up different amounts of space?

What strategies can you use to find which canister has six marbles?

Liquids (Insights)—Second Grade

What do you think you know about liquids?

What can you observe about liquids?

What are the special properties of water, oil, and corn syrup?

How are drops of liquids different?

What happens when you try to mix different liquids together?

Which solids sink and which ones float in water?

How do objects sink or float in oil and corn syrup?

Can you make a sinker float?

What features can make an object float?

What features can make an object sink?

What do you think you know about liquids as well as floaters and sinkers?

Soils (STC)—Second Grade

What do you think you will observe about soil?

What do you think happens to plants after they die? How will the contents of the containers with and without worms change over time?

Using your senses, what can you observe about sand, clay, and humus?

What happens to sand, clay, and humus when they get wet?

How are the smears of the soil components different?

How quickly do different soil components settle in water?

How have the contents of the settling tubes changed?

What soil components do you think are in your mystery mixture? How did the three tests help you make this decision?

Do the healthiest plants grow in sand, clay, or humus?

What happens to roots in different soil?

How does water move through humus? How much water can humus hold?

How does water move through sand and clay? How much water can sand and clay hold?

What happens to plants after they die? What do earthworms do that helps soil and plants?

What do roots do for a plant?

What have we learned in our investigations about sand, humus, and clay that will help us identify what is in our local soil?

Plant Growth and Development (STC) — Third Grade

What can you observe about a dry bean seed?

How has the bean seed changed since it has been soaking?

What might happen to the seeds during the next twenty-four hours?

What differences can you observe in the seedlings?

What do you observe about the plant over time? What do you predict the line of the graph will look like? How tall do you predict the plant will be in the end?

What did you observe during the plant's growth spurt?

What do the different parts of the bee do?

What do you think the different parts of the flower do for the plant?

How do bees and plants help each other?

How are the flowers of the plants changing?

How is a model useful in learning about plants and animals?

What does a model help us to know about plants and bees?

How can we use a model to represent what we have learned about plants and bees?

What story does the graph tell about your plant?

What could you do to the plants to make them produce even more seeds?

Rocks and Minerals (STC) — Third Grade

What do we think we know about rocks? What can we observe about rocks?

How are rocks similar and different?

How are rocks formed?

How are minerals different from rocks?

What properties can you observe and compare in different minerals?

How are minerals similar and different?

How can we determine the identifying color of a mineral?

How can we use simple tools to determine how much light passes through a mineral?

How can we use simple tools to determine how much a mineral's surface reflects light?

How can we use simple tools to determine the hardness of a mineral?

How can we determine if a mineral is magnetic?

What can you observe about the shape of the different minerals?

What properties can you observe and compare in different samples of the same mineral?

How can you use the information gathered in your mineral guide to identify the minerals?

How can you use what you have learned to identify "mystery minerals"?

How are rocks and minerals used?

Sound (STC)—Third Grade

In what ways are the sounds we hear alike and different?

How do you think sound gets from place to place?

In what ways are the sounds that different nails make similar and different?

How does the length of rulers affect pitch?

What patterns can you see and hear in vibrating rulers?

What do you think causes a slide whistle to make different pitches?

What have you learned so far that will help you design a reed instrument?

What can we do to show that sound causes vibrations?

How can we make sounds with strings?

What are the important things to consider in planning your own investigation about how [for example, tension, length, or thickness or gauge of an object] affects vibration and pitch?

In what ways does tightening or loosening a string change the sound it makes?

How does the length of a string affect the sound it makes?

How does the thickness of a string affect the sound it produces?

What can you do to make louder sounds come from the strings?

How does what we know about sound help us understand how our vocal cords work?

How can what we have learned about sound help us make musical instruments?

Circuits and Pathways (Insights)—Fourth Grade

What do you think you already know about electricity and electric circuits?

In what ways can you connect the motor to the D-cell so that the shaft of the motor spins?

What do you think is needed to make a bulb light up?

Where does electricity flow in a bulb?

What path does light travel? What happens to light when it reaches an obstacle?

Which materials allow electric current to flow through and which do not?

What is a closed or complete circuit?

How can you use a circuit tester to determine which brass fasteners are connected by wires?

What happens when you add bulbs to a circuit?

How can you measure the brightness of a bulb?

How can you wire (connect) bulbs in a circuit so that removing one of the bulbs does not make the other bulb(s) in the circuit go out?

What does a switch do in a circuit?

What are the important things to consider in planning your own investigation about resistance?

How does the [length, gauge, type of wire] affect the brightness of the bulb?

What does a fuse do in a circuit?

How can you use a circuit tester to determine what electric component is wired between two brass fasteners?

Ecosystems (STC)—Fourth Grade

How do living things depend on each other?

How do you predict the living and nonliving things in the terrarium will change over time? How might they affect each other?

What are the roles of plants and algae in the aquarium?

What are the roles of animals in the aquarium?

How do the living and nonliving things in the aquarium affect each other?

What are the dependent and interdependent relationships in the terrarium?

How do water and land ecosystems affect each other?

How does pollution made by humans affect the stability of an ecosystem or ecosystems?

What are the important things to consider in planning your own investigation about pollutants?

What similarities and differences are you seeing with your ecocolumns and the control ecocolumn?

Where do the pollutants go?

What are some of the challenges in drawing conclusions about your investigation?

How can groups effectively present solutions to people with different points of view?

Food Chemistry (STC) — Fourth Grade

What do you think you know about the foods you eat?

How can we observe and record our observations of different foods?

What does the positive test result look like for the presence of starch?

How much starch is in the different foods?

What additional information can we find through research of the nutrient? What does this nutrient do for the body? When might you especially need it? Does it come from plants or animals or both? How do you test for this nutrient? What foods that you have tested contain it?

What does the positive test result look like for the presence of glucose?

How much glucose is in the different foods?

What does the positive test result look like for the presence of fats?

How much fat is in the different foods?

What does the positive test result look like for the presence of protein?

How much protein is in the different foods?

What is the function of each part of the digestive system?

How does the information we have from our tests compare with the information found on food labels? What information can we find through research of vitamins?

Why would you take, or not take, marshmallows on a ten-mile hike?

Land and Water (STC)—Fifth Grade

What do you think you know about land and water?

How can using models help us learn about the real world? Where are all the places water can be on our planet and in your model? How does water change in order to do this?

What happens to land as it rains and where does the rain go?

How does a flowing stream change the land?

What are the properties of each type of soil? How does each soil behave in water?

How does the speed of the water affect the amount of soil that is worn away (eroded) and the amount of soil that is dropped off (deposited)?

What are the similarities and differences of the model streams? What are the common parts of all stream systems?

What patterns do you notice when several streams flow over the land?

What are the important things to consider in planning your own investigation about interactions between land and water?

How does greater water flow affect the amount of erosion and deposition? What is the evidence from your model that supports your thinking?

How do landforms affect the direction and flow of water?

How do dams affect streams and rivers?

How does sloped land affect the flow of water and the amount of soil that is eroded and deposited downstream?

Where do you predict the water will flow in your landscape? Support your thinking with evidence from past investigations.

If you were to build your landscape and place your homesites again, what would you do differently? Why?

Microworlds (STC)—Fifth Grade

What is something new you can discover about a penny?

What is the difference between an observation, an inference, and an opinion?

What properties must objects have if they are to be used as magnifiers?

What have you learned about magnifiers?

How are a hand lens and a microscope similar and different?

Using a microscope, what can you learn about how pictures are printed in newspapers and magazines?

How does the field of view change as you get closer to an object? How does it change as the microscope magnifies an object?

Which is the best slide-mounting technique for viewing different objects?

What properties of the four different substances enable you to identify what they are?

How do you think the hay infusion will change over three to four weeks?

How do we know if something is alive?

How can a microscope help us determine if something is alive?

In an organism that is made up of many cells, such as the human body, how are the cells organized?

What can you observe and learn about *Volvox*? Is it alive? Is it a plant, an animal, or what?

What can you observe and learn about *Blepharisma*? Is it alive? Is it a plant, an animal, or what?

What can you observe and learn about vinegar eels? Are they alive? Are they a plant, an animal, or what?

What are all the things an environment needs to provide in order for living things to survive?

Models and Designs (FOSS)—Fifth Grade

What does the inside of the black box look like?

How can building a physical model provide evidence of what the inside of the black box looks like?

How is the humdinger a system? How do its parts (subsystems) depend on each other and work together?

What are the main parts (subsystems) of the go-cart system? How do these parts work together to make the go-cart move?

What are some design problems you have encountered and how have you redesigned your go-cart to solve the problems?

How does wheel size affect the distance a go-cart can travel?